Anna L Boyden

Echoes from Hospital and White House

A record of Mrs. Rebecca R. Pomroy's experience in war-times. Vol. 1

Anna L Boyden

Echoes from Hospital and White House
A record of Mrs. Rebecca R. Pomroy's experience in war-times. Vol. 1

ISBN/EAN: 9783337409296

Printed in Europe, USA, Canada, Australia, Japan

Cover: Foto ©ninafisch / pixelio.de

More available books at **www.hansebooks.com**

MR. LINCOLN VISITS THE HOSPITAL. (*Page* 95.)

ECHOES

FROM

HOSPITAL AND WHITE HOUSE

A RECORD OF MRS. REBECCA R. POMROY'S
EXPERIENCE IN WAR-TIMES

BY
ANNA L. BOYDEN

"In the great history of the land,
A noble type of good, heroic womanhood."

TO THE
LOYAL SOLDIERS OF OUR LAND,
WHO PERILED THEIR LIVES AND THEIR FORTUNES FOR
HOME AND COUNTRY,
THIS LITTLE VOLUME IS SINCERELY AND
RESPECTFULLY DEDICATED

PREFACE.

Through the earnest solicitation of friends, Mrs. Pomroy consents that a portion of her life shall go before the public.

With the increase of years, the natural desire for quiet and seclusion makes it less and less an object of interest on her part, but all the more desirous are friends that the work of collecting and arranging in permanent form the incidents that occurred during her public service, should not be delayed until the channels of information, which grow less with every increasing year, shall be insufficient to furnish material for the work.

This little volume is not intended as a biography; it is simply an eventful chapter out of her history—a leaf from the book of life. A leaf blotted with tears, it is true, yet showing so unmistakably God's guiding hand in every line, and exhibiting the relation between pure motives and noble achievements so clearly as to stimulate rather than depress.

The stirring events of our Civil War, in which

she bore her part so well, are fading from memory. They live in history, it is true, but who shall rehearse the story of those lives offered as a sacrifice on the altar of their country, when this generation shall have passed away?

The lessons taught by their fortitude, valor, and self-sacrifice, are needed for the inspiration and incentive of coming generations.

We regret that our sources of intelligence, with regard to the special events of Mrs. Pomroy's service, are not more ample, particularly that portion of it during which she was a member of President Lincoln's family at the White House. A journal which she had carefully kept during that period, in which she had recorded her most interesting interviews and conversations with the President, was lost during one of her furloughs, and we are thereby deprived of much valuable material.

Personal recollections supply this deficiency in part, which, together with letters and information derived from a few who were privileged to call her "Mother," in the hospital, furnish the chief source of supply from which we obtain our information.   A. L. B.

NEWTON, MASS., 1884.

CONTENTS.

I.

HE LEADETH ME.

Early Widowhood.—Incidents at Hamilton Camp-Meeting.—Beginning of the War.—Her Desire to go as Nurse.—Telegram from Miss Dix.—Arrival in Washington.

II.

FREE TO SERVE.

Youthful Service.—Georgetown Hospital.—First Night's Experience.—Goes to Columbia College Hospital.—Its Appearance and Surroundings.—First Impressions.—Duties as a Nurse.—Letters Home.—Soldiers' Needs.—Nurse's Poetry. Assistance from the North.—Small Pox Scare.—Eleventh Maine Regiment.—The Bugler Boy.—Another Death.—Member of the Band.—First Prayer Meeting.—Sunday at Columbia College.—Ward-Room.—Barnet of Michigan.—Treatment for Scurvy.—Soldiers Encouraged.—Catholic Priest.—The quiet Nurse who carried her Point.

III.

CERTAINLY I WILL BE WITH THEE.

Abraham Lincoln.—Is called to the White House.—Interview with the President.—Letter Home.—Visit to the White House.—False Aspersions corrected.—Obtains Permission for Protestant Service.— Assistance of Washington Friends. — Soldiers' Free Library.— "The Rebel Flags."— Rev. John Pierpont.— Mrs. Secretary Wells.— Ice Cream.— Scarcity of Supplies.— Soldiers' Union Relief Association.— A Cup of Tea.— Miss Gilson.

IV.

ALL MY SPRINGS ARE IN THEE.

Furlough at the White House.— Privations of Soldiers and their Families.— Invoice of wounded Men.— Act of Emancipation.— Incidents of President Lincoln's Life.— "Little Tad." Incident in the Guest Chamber.— Influx of Wounded Men. — Petition for a Chaplain.— Vermont Boy.— A Visit from the President.— Charlemagne.— Skennel.— Letters Home. — Soldiers' Home.

V.

LED ON.

Alarm at Washington.— Visits Virginia.— The Wounded brought in.— Letters Home.— Furlough.— Presentation of Flag.— Christmas. — Emancipation Proclamation. — Winter in the Hospital.— Album Quilt.— McKinney.— Lucrative Positions offered.— Marriage at the Capitol.— Receptions.— Sickness. — Letters from Home.

VI.

OUR FATHER KNOWETH.

Hospital Cares.— Cliftburn Hospital.— St. Aleosus Hospital.— The Fourth of July.— Mrs. Lincoln's Illness.— Interview with the President.— Widow's Request.— Vermont Boy.— Second Furlough.— Loss of Journal.— Letter Home.— Pickled Beets.— L. E. G.— Miss Dix's Orders.— Routine of Hospital Life.— Visit to Virginia.— Invalid Corps.— Gettysburg.

VII.

I AM WITH YOU ALWAY.

Thanksgiving.—Incidents.—Investigation.—Contrabands.—Song of "The Lively Old Lady."—Little Caty.—Preparations for more Patients.—Incidents.—Pennsylvania Boy.—The Dance.

VIII.

FAITHFUL UNTO DEATH.

Exchange of Prisoners.—Goes to West Hospital.—Hospital Horrors.—A Night in the Attic.—Baltimore Boy and Others.—Rebel Officer.—Visit to Fortress Monroe.—Hospital Incidents.—Loss of Matron.—Visit to Virginia.—New York Boy.—Kane of Cambridgeport.

IX.

SHE HATH DONE WHAT SHE COULD.

Third Furlough.—Extract from *Chelsea Telegraph and Pioneer.*—Letters Home.—The Father's Appeal.—Office Seeker.—Thanksgiving Box.—Rebel won over.—Hanging the Stockings.—One more Smoke.—Sickness.—Assassination of the President.—Is honorably Discharged.—Letter from Newburg.—Subsequent Events.

ECHOES FROM HOSPITAL AND WHITE HOUSE.

CHAPTER I.

HE LEADETH ME.

MRS. REBECCA R. POMROY, a brief portion of whose life comes under our notice, became a widow at the age of forty, and under circumstances exceedingly painful.

Her husband had been a sufferer for nineteen years, during which time she had buried a dear brother and sister, a promising son and an only daughter. One son alone remained to her out of that once happy family group. When she parted with her husband, the last of these dear sufferers, all of whom she had watched through weary months of nursing, the fountain of loving service seemed to have exhausted itself, and she felt as one stricken of God. Still another trial was in store for her. The pleasant little home, where had budded and blasted all the fond hopes of wife and mother, must be sold and passed over to the hands of strangers. True, there were friendly hearts and homes opened to receive and assist her, but Rachel's grief, that would not be comforted, was upon her.

Eighteen months had passed, and friends, anxious to bring some change into the weary life, suggested a few days' recreation at Hamilton Camp meeting. After many entreaties she consented, with utter indifference as to its result, to try the remedy that nature stores up for her children in the pine grove, and the change that comes from meeting new faces in new surroundings. Here her comfort and convenience was most kindly consulted. For three days she sat apart, weak and sensitive, only able to commune with her own troubled heart, touched, doubtless, by the sweet melody of the Methodist hymns, wafted in from the surrounding tents and cottages, mingled with the sweet, undefinable influences of life in the forest. At the end of three days there came a terrible thunder-shower.

Torrents of rain fell, and all the ladies in the tent, with the exception of Mrs. Pomroy and an aged Christian lady, took refuge in the hotel not far distant. I make special mention of these slight events because of what follows.

God had evidently, in his good providence, brought her here for a purpose. He had arranged the place and the time when he could so manifest himself to her as to change the whole current of her being and purpose of her life, as the circumstances that follow will show.

Mrs. Pomroy speaks of this experience as follows: "As we sat alone in our tent, this kind, motherly Christian showed great interest in me, telling me in the sweetest tones that my Heavenly Father was doing all things well by me, and that he was only trying me so that I could do more for him than ever before. I said that it was impossible for me to do anything more for any one, and that I wished to die. She then told me to put all my faith on Christ, who was watching over me like a mother over a sick child, and try to say, 'Lord, do with me as thou thinkest best, but hold up my goings,' and I should gain strength. She prayed earnestly for me, and I gave up all into his hands. For the first time for years I slept soundly that night. I woke, after that beautiful slumber, refreshed and thrilled with a sense of the goodness of God in the physical world about me, and felt as though I never had loved him as I did then. My great grief that had lain so long like a heavy burden was rolled away, and my heart said continually, 'Bless the Lord, O my soul.' I was the first one out at the morning meeting, and the first one to speak of God's love. From that time I continued to improve. Appetite, strength and spirits came back, and when Saturday came, and the meetings broke up, I was loath to leave. When I first trod those grounds my harp was hung on the willows, but now the voice of the Spirit seemed to say, 'Go home, and tell thy friends what great things the Lord hath done for thee.' That night, on parting with the aged Christian, she remarked, 'The Lord has a work for you to do, and he will strengthen you for it.' From this time forth my mind gained in quietude and health, bodily strength came back by degrees, and I began to wonder if the Lord had not something more for me to do."

Two years of widowhood had now passed when

the cry of war agitated our nation. Husbands and sons were enlisting, or mustering in camp, or, already on the field of action, were pouring out their hearts' blood, or, rescued from the battle-field, were languishing in impromptu hospitals from insufficient treatment and nursing. With the call for men came the call for nurses. One day Mrs. Pomroy took up the daily paper to peruse the war record, when her eye scanned one of those advertisements for nurses, common enough in the papers at that period, and her attention was arrested. She read and re-read, and with every perusal strength of purpose grew within her. The pulse beat quickly as she thought, "I can answer these requirements; what is to hinder my going? No earthly tie keeps me back, for my son, the only one left of all my family treasures, is already on the battle-field. Lord, what wilt thou have me to do?" Nerved by prayerful faith, her purpose is no sooner matured than she seeks an interview with the old family physician, and tells him her wish to go to Washington. Here she encounters the first of a series of obstacles. Her old friend, Doctor Forsyth, replied, "You cannot endure, in your present state of health, such a long journey, with the coarse food and foul air that must be your portion in those dreadful hospitals.

Her answer was, "I want to be a mother to those wounded and dying soldiers." Hon. Frank B. Fay, then mayor of Chelsea, had just returned from Washington, where he was engaged in service in hospitals and on the battle-field, and she was advised to confer with him. She did so, telling him how much her heart was set upon the object before her. His advice was of a similar nature. He said the rations of salt pork, meal, and government beef would be insupportable; that they would not take such a frail-looking woman. In addition, he said there were already one thousand women whose names were registered in books at the State House, waiting their orders, and they would be sent for first. She then told him of her special preparation for the work; the nineteen years of nursing in a sick room, and how she thought the Lord had called her to go, adding that she should not have her name on those books, but should write directly to Miss Dix, and trust the result to her Heavenly Father. The parting words of Mayor Fay furnished little encouragement, but, true to the fact that obstacles prove only incentives to the determined spirit, she went to a third friend, who thought, she says, "that I must be a little insane," to dream of so laborious a work.

But at last she found one, an old friend of her husband's, Mr. D. of Somerville, whose face lighted up as she told him her story. He thought she had better sleep over it one more night, and in the morning he would talk with her again. The morning dawned and the conversation was renewed, at the conclusion of which he said, "I do say go, and the Lord go with you. Write your letter on the spot to Miss Dix." She did so. This was on Thursday. On the following Sunday she received a message from Miss Dix, superintendent of female — nurses, requesting her to report on Tuesday at Washington. The telegram was announced in the various churches of Chelsea Sunday morning, and that evening the usual preaching services were exchanged for meetings of prayer and supplication on her behalf.

Mrs. Pomroy's long residence in Chelsea had brought her into pleasant relations with a large circle of friends, and, for a period of years, hers was known as the "afflicted family;" and when she appeared among that assembly of friends, in the large Congregational church, that Sunday evening, to exchange farewells, as the first volunteer nurse of Chelsea, there was no end of the heartfelt sympathy and prayers offered for her. There were many tears and much handshaking, in the midst of which she broke away to snatch a few hours of rest before her departure.

Everything being in readiness, Mrs. Pomroy started alone on her journey, Monday morning, late in the month of September, 1861, and reported herself on Tuesday at Miss Dix's headquarters in Washington.

Here her accommodations were of the most meagre kind. She was received by a temporary matron, who informed her that Miss Dix was away on the battle-field. There was nothing in the building to eat, and nothing with which to make a fire. Cold water was the only refreshment offered to the weary traveller, and she went supperless to bed.

On Wednesday morning Miss Dix made her appearance. She received the new-comer pleasantly, asked a few questions, then taking a carriage, they visited places of interest, stopping at Georgetown Hospital.

Finding that a nurse there had been worn out by constant care and watching, she at once decided to leave Mrs. Pomroy to fill the vacancy.

>My heart was hot and restless,
>　And my life was full of care,
>And the burden laid upon me
>　Seemed greater than I could bear.
>
>But now it has fallen from me,
>　It is buried in the sea;
>And only the sorrow of others
>　Throws its shadow over me.

CHAPTER II.

FREE TO SERVE.

OF work as of greatness, it may be said, some are born workers, some become workers, and some have their work thrust upon them.

Mrs. Pomroy was a born worker. From early childhood she was never content unless she was doing something for others. At the age of twelve, during the summer vacations, it was her delight to gather the small children of the neighborhood, keeping them two or three hours, amusing them by reading, playing games, and gathering flowers. Caring for children and making them happy was her highest ambition, and so successful was she that parents felt relief and satisfaction while the little ones were in her charge. At the age of sixteen, she became an active member of the Sunday-school connected with Father Taylor's Seamen's Bethel. It was her practice to visit the families of the poor seamen, invite the wives and children to church and Sunday-school, and when they were destitute, provide suitable clothing, not unfrequently soliciting money to procure boots and shoes in which they could appear respectable. She continued in this labor of love until her marriage called her away. The years that followed were filled with cares and responsibilities, such as many a more hardy woman might reasonably have shrunk from. Now, as the arduous duties of hospital life opened before her, it was evident that she lacked no qualification and was equal to the occasion, except as bodily weakness triumphed over the willing spirit. Her first experience in Georgetown Hospital we will give in her own words:

"I was put at once on duty in a ward with fifty typhoid patients, and what with the odor and moans of the dying, it did seem to me unbearable. As the surgeon came round about four o'clock to tell me about the medicines, I felt such a faintness that I had to be excused and go to my room. After partaking of water and throwing myself on a miserable little cot, struggling with this dreadful weakness, the familiar words, "He that putteth his hand to the plough and looketh back," broke in upon my distress, and from my heart of hearts I asked the Lord to strengthen me for all that awaited me. And that prayer was heard, for I was obliged to sit up a part of that night, as the soldiers were all tired out. After I resumed duty, while passing several rooms, what should greet my ear but the sound of a sick man's voice calling my name. In surprise, I went to his bedside, and he burst into tears, crying, 'What sent you here?' and grasping my hand, he told me his history. He was a Chelsea boy, by the name of Stevens; had known me in that city, and used frequently to play in my garden with my dear Willie. He had afterwards removed to Boston, and had enlisted from there early in the war. The fatigue and hardships incident to the battle of Bull Run had resulted in dysentery and other weaknesses which soon carried him off. While I was there I gave him all the time I could spare, talked and read to him, and, to use his own expression, 'it did his very soul good to see a woman from home whom he had never expected to see again.' . . .

"In a little room by himself lay a sick boy who had been dying several hours. His frequent calls for his mother were heart-rending. I watched and soothed him, gave him the last stimulant, when he put his arms around my neck, crying, 'Oh, my dear mother!' and died. I had to call one of the watch to release me from the death grasp, then another, and not till after a hard struggle did they succeed. My first night in a hospital! I can never forget it, and how I was sustained.

"On the next bed I visited lay a young man who had had a ball pass through his wrist, and was suffering exceedingly, not only mentally but physically. He was eighteen years of age, and had enlisted without his mother's consent. He would not let her know where he was, for 'it would break her heart,' he said. He was all she had. During the days that followed I read and talked to him, and advised him to let me write to that widowed mother, who lived in Methuen; but 'No,' said he, 'I shall kill my mother.' Soon the litter came to take that dear young man into the operating room, where his hand was amputated. He burst into tears on his return as he took my hand in his remaining one, saying how much I reminded him of his mother."

These are only a few of the many touching incidents that occurred during her stay at the Georgetown Hospital. The following Monday she received orders from Miss Dix to repair to Columbia College Hospital, where she was enrolled as a nurse.

The hospital was situated on Meridian Hill, on the outskirts of the city of Washington, beautifully laid out with driveways, trees, and a fine park in the rear of the building. At the time of the civil outbreak it was the seat of a flourishing Baptist college. From here Doctors Stowe, Neale, and other men of talent, had graduated years before, when it was in possession of the South. Now, seized by government and used as a military hospital, it had assumed a warlike appearance, sadly out of keeping with its original design. At the time of Mrs. Pomroy's entrance, ten regiments were stationed around the building as a protection against the secessionists who had threatened to burn it. At night-time drums beat, bands of music made the air vocal with national and home melodies, while the four outlying hospitals and scores of tents gave a festive appearance to the scene, contrasting sadly with the groans of the dying, the moans of the wounded and the crazy paroxysms of typhoid patients within.

We extract portions of a letter written soon

after Mrs. Pomroy entered the hospital, which give a somewhat detailed account of how she found things, and her first impressions, dated October 12.

DEAR SISTER H.—It is Saturday night, and I am sitting in one of my pleasantest rooms, watching over several of my boys. You can have no idea of their suffering, even if I should attempt to describe it. In the next room are two handsome young men, unconscious of suffering, who have been dying all night, and we are ignorant about their friends, as they came to us so delirious that they knew nothing. We always get their names if possible when the ambulance brings them in, that we may telegraph to their friends. When they are brought in they are carried to the bath room, stripped entirely and washed thoroughly; then they are put into bed and the clothing they wore is rolled up, after the money, photographs and the like, are taken from their pockets, their name marked on their bundle, then, with the sword and knapsack, it is put in a shed, on a shelf, until called for. Many of our patients are dying of typhoid. Their tongues are black and their breath is extremely offensive. While I am writing, a New York company is doing escort duty for one who was a patient of mine, who is to be buried to-morrow. As many of my boys ask me the name of their dead mates, I take the opportunity to speak to them of their need of preparation for the same change, and they always listen with great attention. I have become familiar with death. Often I am called at the solemn hour of midnight to stand alone by the bedside of the dying, and close mouth and eyes. Many have died clasping my hand tightly. O, dear sister, will you ask every friend of mine to pray for the dying soldier? The prayers he utters for wife or mother are often heart-rending, but I cannot talk to him, for his ears are past all sound. I feel that I am placed in a very trying situation. How could I do what I am called to if I was not strengthened by an unseen hand and fed daily and hourly with the bread of heaven? . . . . . Our rations are twenty cents a day, one dollar and forty cents a week. That money is put into beef, bread, rice, etc., and we all go in together and get one of our sick soldiers to cook for us. Of course it is cooked man-fashion. We are not allowed to bake bread, cake or pies, but must live like the camp. 'We work like slaves — work all day and part of the night,' is all I hear from the nurses. But I get along very nicely, as I have tea occasionally from home, and with that and what Miss Dix sends us, I feel that I have no reason to complain. 'A contented mind is a continual feast.' I am very happy in mind, still have hold of my Saviour's hand, and believe he has yet a great work for me to do. They have put me to blistering all the patients under my care, who have typhoid, and you must know it is no pleasant task to perform for so many soldiers morning and evening; but they think I do just right and the physicians give me much credit. There are some among our number who drank from the spring water poisoned by the rebels. Two of our men have already died from the effects of it. Our nurses are ten in all. Two each from Ohio, New York, Connecticut, Pennsylvania and Massachusetts. We all dress just as we please; not, however, without regard to Miss Dix's expressed opinion. She says 'she expects a nurse will dress according to her work.' We are not allowed out of the hospital even to walk on the grounds. We are under government rule, surely. . . . .

I want the good ladies of Chelsea to knit some thick socks for our sick and wounded. Our windows are open night and day, and they all complain of the cold. I would like some postage stamps for the sick men when they write home, also a boiled ham, as we can eat that without cooking; and some crackers, as the sick men cannot eat the poor bread. Your hearts would ache could you see two hundred half-starved men getting up from the fever. Boxes of fruit, jellies and cologne often come to the nurses of our hospital from strangers, and I always give my part to my boys. I have twenty-seven men, and to-day they had six grapes apiece, and you should see how they snatched at them. I am obliged to cut an orange into eight pieces for those who cannot speak a word or eat a particle of food. If some of the good people of Chelsea will make up a box for the soldiers who are so anxious to get well and join their regiments, they will be grateful, I assure you, and take up their duties on the field again with a will. My love to all.
                                                              R. R. POMROY.

The people of that city were not backward in responding to this appeal, for early in December she writes, "I have received six boxes from Chelsea, and the contents has been distributed in the best manner possible. Could Mrs. L. have seen the grateful smiles with which her gift of the grapes and wine were received, she would have felt amply repaid.

"Thirteen of my soldier boys went to the convalescent hospital in Baltimore, last week. Some of them, when sent here, had been given over by their physicians, but God blessed the means used for their recovery, and they were able to leave and make room for sicker patients. As they each took my hand to say Good-by, they said they should never forget that name, Chelsea, and when the war was over, if their lives were spared, they would find out more about the place, by visiting it." She speaks farther of receiving short visits from Reverend Doctor M., Messrs. B. and S., and Mayor Fay, all from there, and sends the following bit of poetry, written by one of her fellow nurses:

>What do we live for?
>Live to be nurses,
>Watching sick soldiers at Columbia Hall;

Soothing their heartaches,
Stilling their curses,
Breathing a prayer to the Father of all.

What do we live for?
Live for the mothers
Who send their brave sons at Liberty's call,
To die on the battlefield,
Or, living as brothers,
Here claiming our kindness, given to all.

What do we live for?
Live for the sisters
Whose glory and pride we find in our camps,
Who, sick with the fever,
We poultice and blister,
Returning them weekly in health to the ranks.

What do we live for?
The wives and the maidens
Whose patriot duty is staying at home,
Earnestly praying
That with victory laden,
Husband and lover with Union will come.

From another letter, dated December 31, we quote the following: "As I take a glance at my patients, and hear the moan of distress and the sharp cry of suffering, I often wish that friends could look in and see how carefully our boys are watched and their wants attended to by faithful nurses. It is not all sad either. We have our reward, not in dollars and cents, but in the looks of satisfaction that prevail. Kind words at the outset often drive away the patient's fears on coming into the hospital. . . . .

"During the three months I have been here I have received seven boxes from Chelsea, two from Newton Corner, one from G. P. Smith of Boston, one from the West Newton Congregational Church, and one from the Tremont Street Methodist. Up to this time I have received eighty-six letters. To the most important I have endeavored to reply, and to write for my boys to their afflicted friends, which makes in all one hundred and twenty-two letters. . . . .

"Two weeks since I had notice to prepare beds for twenty-six patients sick with measles. It was heartsickening to see how many of them came up to my ward, helpless, upon litters. They were of the Eleventh Maine, all of them fine, stout men when they left home. One of them cried out on seeing me, 'What will my poor mother say when I am laid away from her?' One of my measley boys, after getting through with it, was taken down with small-pox. I was ordered to take care of him alone all one night, till the surgeon in charge came, and then such excitement! The man was sent to the small-pox hospital, and order was given for his nurse to be vaccinated without delay, then to commence at the top of the building and vaccinate all the patients. I have a very lame arm, and shall be sure of one scar to remind me of my college days. As a result of the exposure, a boy was soon stricken down with small-pox. Our Sabbath was all confusion and excitement. The patient was kept in our midst till Monday noon, then carried to the small-pox hospital, perhaps to die like the one I cared for, who lived only a few hours after I gave him the parting hand."

When the Eleventh Maine boys were brought in with measles, they were under quarantine, as was their attendant. She could only go from the sick ward to her meals. The disease made great havoc in the regiment, more than one hundred dying out of it. Among all the men who came under her care, none were so strictly temperate as the Eleventh Maine. The surgeons insisted that they should be stimulated with wine and brandy, but many totally refused it. One little fellow said to Mrs. Pomroy, "I'll die sooner than take it, for I promised my mother that I would not take a drop." He lived, while as a rule, those who took stimulants died.

Among these Maine boys was the bugler of the regiment. Wasting away, week by week, the poor fellow had become a mere skeleton. It was evident that his hours were numbered, and when he became conscious of the fact, he called for Mrs. Pomroy and said, "Mother, can I have my bugle?"

She immediately despatched an attendant to get an order from the surgeon on the ward to have it brought up. The beloved bugle was found, brightly burnished, and given to the dying boy. Too weak to hold it in his emaciated and nerveless hands, it was sustained by the attendant and put to his lips.

As he concentrated the little energy left in his poor weak body for the final effort, while his face brightened and the old fire came into his eye, two or three weak strains wavered and died away like echoes of the lofty tones that once breathed through it, his hands fell, the breath ceased, and the last bugle call had been sounded.

Mrs. Pomroy writes at the commencement of the year 1862 as follows:

"The first day of January was ushered in by a "Happy New Year" from nearly all my boys. As I entered my room quite early in the morning, and passed from one bed to another, I felt there were some who would stay but a few days to enjoy the new year.

"On the third morning I was called to the bedside of my youngest boy, who had a very sick night, and, as he took hold of my hand, asked me if I thought he would ever get well. There had been a marked change during the night, and I had my fears that he would not live through the day. I told him he was very sick, and asked him if there was anything I could do for him.

"'If I could see my dear mother and my little sister Lucy only once more, I should be happy.'

"The tears fell thick and fast, and there was a struggle. After he got calmer he asked me to read from the Bible, which I did, and then complied with his request for prayer. He then fell asleep, and I left him to go to my three other very sick men, whose time with us was short. When I came to his bedside again, he awoke and told me he had dreamed that he had seen the Saviour, who told him that he would take him to Heaven that day. He called all the boys round him, told them to prepare to meet him in Heaven, and bade them all good-by as though he were going on some pleasant journey. I shall never forget the sweetness of his face as he said:

> Jesus can make a dying bed
> Feel soft as downy pillows are,

and, 'Good-by, Nurse! we shall meet again.' I cannot tell you the gratitude he expressed for all that had been done for him. A few minutes before he died he desired his nurse to take one hand in hers and place her other upon his heart until it ceased to beat.

"'Tell my *other* mother when you write, that you felt my last heart throb.'

"Soon after he cried out, 'Glory to God in the highest! I'm going home.' Dear boy! just as our evening candles were lighted, his spirit took its departure where there is no need of light, even of the sun or moon. It was Saturday evening, and my sweet-faced little soldier was carried from my sight to the home for the dead. I returned to my chamber and wept.

"I was soon summoned to the bedside of another who was not expected to live through the night. His last request was to be sent home to his friends, and he had given me his final farewell. He belonged to the same regiment, and was a member of the band. His death was peaceful and happy, and the music of earth was exchanged for that of Heaven. Two days after, another left me. He was peaceful and trusting, and requested me to look after his clothing and keepsakes, and to write to his wife and two sweet children, telling them he should never see them more on earth, but asking them to prepare to meet him in Heaven. The next day — and must I tell the sad tale? — my fourth boy (all of the Eleventh Maine) called me to his bedside and said, 'You have been the only mother I have had since I left home. May God bless you in this world and in the world to come, for being such a good friend to us poor soldiers. God bless you!' fell again from his lips — the last words he spoke.

"These first two weeks of the new year have witnessed much suffering and death. Great credit is due the colonel of the Eleventh Maine regiment, as he visited my boys twice a day, and brought in the surgeon of his regiment to see if anything more could be done for those who were struggling hard for life.

"On Saturday afternoon the nurses and attendants rode to the station to follow the remains of a dear young man who had been an attendant since July, in the hospital. He was unusually polite and refined, very kind to the sick — was with them night and day, always wearing a smiling face. His nurse thought there was none like James. He had been her patient, and on his partial recovery had been detailed as her attendant. A week's sickness, and the clergyman's only son was called away to a higher service. How we all sympathized with our Massachusetts nurse, who wept for him like a sister for a brother.

"Two gentlemen from Boston called Sabbath evening, and, for the first time, we had a prayer and praise meeting. Forty boys were present, two physicians and five nurses. It seemed homelike to our boys as the familiar hymns were sung from the Soldier's Hymn Book, and it was a season of refreshing for us nurses to have anything of the kind in which we could participate. Among the number who took part were two of the soldiers, who spoke earnestly to their fellow-comrades. .... The first Sunday in January I was awakened by the band playing *Nellie Gray* and *Dixie*, and at eight o'clock our national flag was raised in front of the hospital."

Sunday was usually a gala day at Columbia College. All the regiments appeared on dress parade, and the bands played all the popular national airs. In the near distance sparkled the blue Potomac in the sunshine, making it a scene from Mrs. Pomroy's front window never to be forgotten by the invalid soldier. Within the room her thoughtful sympathy created an atmosphere in their midst which was truly a Sabbath benediction.

Their baths were taken the night before, and they were dressed in clean linen, hair and beards were trimmed by the barber, their beds supplied with fresh sheets and white spreads, while clean white handkerchiefs, scented with cologne, were put in the hands of each invalid. Then, after attending to their several wants, she would take the Bible, and with the reading combine many tender applications, much motherly advice and comfort that went straight to the hearts of her soldier boys. As the day wore on, those who were able wrote letters to the home friends, or read from the books and papers with which they were amply supplied.

Mrs. Pomroy's room was an upper one, the largest and pleasantest among them all, and accommodated thirty patients. The large bay-window was kept filled with house-plants, the table in the centre held "mother's" work-box, for the boys wanted it there to make the place seem homelike. Here she taught them to sew and mend their stockings, and here, when time passed heavily with the impatient convalescents, they beguiled the weary hours at a game of dominoes. Thirty pictures, the gift of thoughtful friends, decorated the walls. A favorite one for study and reflection was a fine one of "Pilgrim's Progress." "Maud Muller" was another favorite with the boys.

Several among the New York Zouaves, who had been in the habit of decorating churches, had ornamented the walls with evergreen mottoes. Among the number were, "Our Boys in Blue," "Gettysburg," "We honor the Brave" and the like. No pains was spared by Mrs. Pomroy to make the surroundings of her patients as attractive and homelike as possible. Governor Andrew, coming in one day, remarked on the cleanliness and taste of the surroundings, and said, "If I were sick I should like to come here and lie." She was known as "the mother who loved her boys;" and it was no wonder they gave her their confidence and loyal devotion in return.

Among those who regarded her with the deepest gratitude was one Barnet, belonging to the Black Horse Cavalry of Michigan. For weeks he had languished with typhoid. One night the surgeon on his rounds said it was useless to do anything more for him. "He will not last till morning; don't sit up wasting your strength over him; you are foolish to spend so many sleepless nights with your boys." His two brothers, officers in the same regiment, had been in to look upon him for the last time. But something told his nurse to make one more effort for the dying man. Already the cold, clammy sweat that precedes death was upon him. A faint flutter of the heart was the only sign of life. Mrs. Pomroy went to her stores for milk and wine, prepared a punch and put a teaspoonful to his lips.

She waited a few minutes, saw that his heart still feebly pulsated, and that his extremities were slightly warmer, and gave another spoonful, meanwhile applying hot flannels and a jug of hot water to his feet. She was rewarded by seeing, with repeated applications, warmth and animation returning. The surgeon on his morning rounds expected to find him dead, and said, "What have you been doing to him, Nurse?"

She told him what she had done, thinking that he was so near death that it could at least do him no harm. He said, "That's right; keep on, and I think he'll pull through!" And so he did. His term of convalescence ended in a few weeks, and he was granted a furlough.

She says, on relating the incident, "I never expected to see my Michigan boy again; but one day, three years afterwards, on getting into a crowded horse car, coming from Baltimore, a a fine-looking soldier, with shoulder-straps, beckoned me across the car to take his seat. Weak and weary, I was only too glad to do so, when he stood erect before me, saying, 'Mother, don't you know me?' I said 'no: are you one of my soldier boys?' 'Yes,' he replied, 'I'm Barnet, whom the doctor gave up; I owe my life to you.'

I never shall forget the animation of his fine, manly face and figure as he poured forth his gratitude to me in that crowded horse car, told me how he had become a Christian while under my care, had, on his recovery, married the girl of his heart, and had come back to be promoted and serve his country to the end."

Another young fellow, transferred to Mrs. Pomroy's ward from Washington, was so reduced by army exposure as to be very sick, and supposed to be dying of consumption. For weeks his patient nurse had watched the ebb and flow of life, till there seemed to be little or nothing to build hope upon. The surgeon finally said, "He is past all help. Don't give him any more medicine; his time is short." The poor fellow's mouth was raw with scurvy.

One day he called his nurse and said, "Mother, I want some pickle. Can't I have some?" Touched with what seemed his last request, she despatched her attendant to Washington for a jar of them. She cut half a pickle into little pieces and fed him with it, reasoning within herself, "He cannot live without it, and he can no more than die if I give it to him."

She found him alive the next morning, anxious for more pickle, and she gave him half of another. He seemed to grow brighter and stronger, and she gave him a whole one the next day. Whether it was the pickles, or some other unknown agency, God blessed the means of recovery to this poor boy, and he was able to be sent to the Convalescent Hospital shortly after, from whence he joined his regiment.

These are only some of the many instances in which Mrs. Pomroy saved the lives of men given over by their physicians. There was something in her calm courage and sweet, womanly sympathy, that imparted life-giving energy to these forlorn, despairing men. An instance in point was the case of a badly wounded soldier who, for the first time, was brought into a hospital. All hope had faded out of his heart when he learned that he was to be carried to that dreadful place where life was estimated to be held so cheap. His two companions took him upon a stretcher and laid him upon his bed in Mrs. Pomroy's ward, where he burst into tears. "Here, Jim," he said, "take my watch, I sha'n't need it any more. Take all my things, for I sha'n't stay *here* long."

At this Mrs. Pomroy stooped over him and said, "Now, my boy, look here, you are going to get well. Most all the boys in my ward do, and I'll do all I can for you. Don't give up your watch; you'll want it in a little while, it will be so much company for you. I'll take care of it, with your money and your photographs, and you shall have them again when you want them."

For the first time he regarded her with a look of interest, and said, "Have you got a boy?" "Yes," she answered, "and he's on the battle-field. I expect him to be brought to me at any time."

With that the light came into his beautiful blue eyes; his voice gathered strength as he remarked to his comrades, "Well, I'll let you keep the watch and things. Come round and see me in a day or two, and I'll try and weather it." Every day for a week or more the boys came round. The third day they found him bright and cheerful. His wounds were doing well, and his watch was his constant companion. The luxury of a nurse with a son on the battle-field, who came round and bade him "good-night" as mother used to, was what he had not expected. He was soon able to join his regiment.

With all the sad sights and sounds incident to hospital life, many, a rare bit of fun or joke at one another's expense, took off the keen edge of homesickness that beset the soldier when he was convalescing. The following instance is one of many.

During the first few months of Mrs. Pomroy's sojourn in Columbia College, Catholic priests were the only spiritual advisers and comforters allowed there, as the surgeon general, most of the physicians and stewards, were Catholics. Consequently, they were allowed ingress at any time. It had been the custom of one of these priests to come into the college weekly to hear confession, and to anoint the dying boys if there were any Catholics, or others who would permit it.

Late one Saturday afternoon he made his appearance in Mrs. Pomroy's ward, altogether the worse for liquor. He was a man sixty years old. His apparel was doubtless contraband, for he wore a battered stove-pipe hat, and an old, faded green overcoat. His shoes were so large for him that they clattered on the floor at each step, while his dilapidated gold-headed cane rattled an accompaniment as he swaggered across the room, much to the amusement of the boys who, as many as were able, propped themselves up on one elbow to see what was going to be done.

He inquired of the nurse if any were going to die. She told him that one or two were near their end, one of whom she was standing over at the time. Thereupon he said he was going to prepare him, and with his unsteady fingers, attempted to cross the boy's hands upon his breast, taking up a tumbler of water that stood by, for the purpose of baptizing him.

"That is not holy water," said Mrs. Pomroy, "it's the water he has been drinking from."

Nothing daunted, the priest seized a basin of

water, nearly upsetting it in his shaking hand.

"That is not holy water; he has just been washed in it," said Mrs. Pomroy, "and besides, my boys are all Protestants, and don't wish to be baptized." "He must be, or he won't go to Heaven," said the priest, growing very red and excited. "I cannot allow it," said she. "I am here to be a mother to these boys. I stand here in their mothers' places, and not one of them would wish to have it done."

The priest, by this time, had worked himself up into a fever of passion, and exclaimed, "I'll have yer expelled! I'll have yer expelled!" But what with the determined manner of the nurse and his own inability to hold himself or anything else steady, he gave over the contest with this threat, and left the room shaking with passion, while the boys shook with laughter.

As he closed the door, a voice shouted, "Mother has gained the victory! Three cheers for our mother!" The feeling of triumph, however, soon gave way to alarm, for the Catholic tendencies of officers in charge were well known.

"You'll surely have to leave," they said to

Mrs. Pomroy. "Well," she replied, "I have done only my duty, and I'll leave the consequences to my Heavenly Father." But there were strong presumptions for supposing that she would be expelled for disobeying orders, and with some trepidation she awaited the consequences, commencing to pack her trunk for the expected removal.

The next day the surgeon in charge, from Washington, and his staff of inspecting officers, were expected on their usual Sunday round. The floor, the beds, and the men were looking their best, and she sat reading to her boys as though nothing unusual was anticipated. To her great surprise, however, the surgeon in charge walked in at the head of his force, smiling very graciously, and saying, "How's the Happy Family this morning?" They complimented her on the neatness of her ward, expressed their satisfaction with everything, and went out without once referring to the ominous subject. There was rejoicing and congratulation among the boys and nurse on their departure.

Mrs. Pomroy was frequently spoken of as

the "quiet nurse," not simply on account of her gentle, restful demeanor among the sick, but for the manner in which she resisted all attempts to be drawn into idle contentions with her fellow-officers. She was, notwithstanding, firm and fearless in a matter of principle, and was none the less known as the woman who always carried her point. Among the many grades of officers and employees of the hospital, there was often wrangling and brow-beating, the shoulder-straps generally carrying the day. Many a poor attendant, or humble nurse, lost his or her position from seeing or exposing too much of the injustice done to the helpless soldier through theft and bribery. It is a well-known and disgraceful fact that many a hospital and sanitary official made himself wealthy at the expense of sick and dying men under his charge.

Mrs. Pomroy had been in the hospital three months, and during that time their daily rations from the mess room included a poor quality of beef for dinner, hard-bread, and a miserable grade of tea and coffee. Forty hungry convalescents were getting up from typhoid, and her private stores, sent by Chelsea friends and others, went but little ways toward affording relief among so many. She drew from her own personal resources that she might obtain delicacies that they craved, but there was much grumbling and dissatisfaction for the want of more and better meat.

Finally an intelligent, outspoken Massachusetts boy said: "I know we are being cheated out of our allowance, for we are entitled by government to a certain amount of meat for each day, and if we can't get it, I will write on to Boston to Governor Andrew and see if something cannot be done."

Mrs. Pomroy despatched an orderly for the book containing Army and Navy Regulations, and there ascertained the truth of his assertion. Thereupon she determined to act. Obtaining an order from the attendant surgeon, she sent her assistant down to the steward, asking if her boys could have meat for breakfast. The steward, indignant, said, "Mrs. Pomroy can't have it; it's not allowed. She is the most extravagant nurse we have."

Nothing daunted, she made application to the surgeon in charge. He received her very graciously, having just partaken of his own midday meal. She told him of the necessities of her convalescent patients, and asked him if government did not allow —— ounces of meat per day. He evinced some embarrassment, said that "he believed there was a provision somewhere of that kind, but the number to be fed was so large, and the army expenses so great, that it was impossible to furnish it."

"But," said she, "is there not an appropriation of money intended to cover it?"

The fact could not be denied, and he said evasively, "If it is supplied to your ward, it will have to be given to all the rest."

"And why should it not be?" she questioned. "They need it as well as mine. Doctor," she continued, "there are some pretty smart boys in my ward, who think there is more than one officer engaged in defrauding them of their just dues, and if the thing is not righted soon, something will be done about it." Here the doctor became very pliable, and said that there should be no further trouble. He gave orders to the steward that day, and the next morning the welcome odor of fried steak surprised the inmates of Columbia College.

She was known among the patients thereafter, as "the woman who got us the beef."

If sweet below
To minister to those whom God doth love,
What will it be to minister above!

CHAPTER III.

CERTAINLY I WILL BE WITH THEE.

WE now come to that period in Mrs. Pomroy's life which brought her into close relationship with the beloved head of the nation, Abraham Lincoln. Universal interest centres around this portion of her history, for through her familiar intercourse with him and his family we get into closer relationship with the inner workings of his mind and heart, only the results of which are known to the world at large.

At the time of which we write, the affairs of the nation lay heavy upon his heart.

Nearly a year had passed since the commencement of the war, and though the Federal forces had gained some valuable points, no deadly blow had been struck at the rebellion. Congress was getting restive under the inactivity of the army in front of the Capitol. The country at large was equally impatient that McClellan had accomplished so little. The President needed all the firmness that he could command to stand at the helm, give the country confidence and courage and parry the blows of his own party as well as those of the enemy.

In the midst of all this a most distressing grief had settled upon his household.

His second son, Willie, was taken sick, and after a brief illness breathed his last. His youngest son was expected to die at any hour, and Mrs. Lincoln was lying sick in bed.

When Miss Dix called to see what aid she could render the unhappy household, the physicians were advising that "Little Tad" and Mrs. Lincoln have better attendance, as there was no one to care for them but Mr. Lincoln and poor old aunt Mary, a colored nurse, formerly a slave in the family of Jeff Davis. The President asked Miss Dix if she could recommend to him a good nurse. She told him there was one out of her corps of nurses that she thought would give him perfect satisfaction. On inquiry, she told him it was Mrs. Pomroy. "Oh, yes," he said, "I have heard of her; will you get her for me?"

Miss Dix's carriage was in attendance, and she immediately drove to Columbia College, and told the surgeon in charge that she was going to take one of his nurses to the White House. The surgeon expressed his regret, but could not do otherwise than give his consent, and Mrs. Pomroy was summoned. She remonstrated with Miss Dix on the score of her inefficiency; with a plea for the sick men under her care, some of whom had only a few days of life allotted them. But it was of no use. She was under military rule, and was only given ten minutes to get ready.

To the boys, who exclaimed with one voice, "Don't leave us, Nurse," she gave the parting hand, adjusted the pillows of those near death for the last time, and left with Miss Dix for the White House.

This sudden and unlooked-for experience filled her mind with strange and sorrowful apprehensions, and the tears coursed down her face as she thought "Oh, if I could only have staid with my boys!" But Miss Dix said, "Dear child, you don't know what the Lord has in store for you. Others can look after your boys, but I have chosen you out of two hundred and fifty nurses to make yourself useful to the head of the nation. What a privilege is yours!"

On their arrival they visited the Green Room, where Willie's remains lay in state, and then passed on to the President's chamber, where Mrs. Lincoln was lying sick, the President sitting beside her. He gave her a warm grasp of the hand, and said, "I am heartily glad to see you, and feel that you can comfort us and the poor sick boy." She was soon taken to the sick room of little Tad, introduced to the two physicians who sat in the hall just outside his door, who before leaving gave directions regarding medicine and treatment for every half-hour in the night.

At half-past six the President came in and invited her down to dine with him; but she kept her station by the bedside of the little sufferer, who lay tossing with typhoid, and at intervals weeping for his dear brother Willie, "who would never speak to him any more." The President came in about ten o'clock, sat down on the opposite side of the bed, and commenced inquiries. "Are you Miss or Mrs.? What of your family?"

She says, "I told him I had a husband and two children in the other world, and a son on the battle-field." "What is your age? What prompted you to come so far to look after these poor boys?" She told him of her nineteen years' education in the school of affliction, and that after her loved ones had been laid away, and the battle-cry had been sounded, nothing remained but for her to go, so strong was her desire. "Did you always feel that you could say, 'Thy will be done?'"

And here the father's heart seemed agonized for a reply.

She said, "No; not at the first blow, nor at the second. It was months after my affliction that God met me when at a camp-meeting."

Here he showed great interest, and, she says, "While I was telling him my history, and, above all, of God's love and care for me through it all, he covered his face with his hands while the tears streamed through his fingers. Then he told me of his dear Willie's sickness and death. In walking the room, he would say: 'This is the hardest trial of my life. Why is it? Oh, why is it?' I tried to comfort him by telling him there were thousands of prayers going up for him daily. He said, 'I am glad of that.' Then he gave way to another outburst of grief.

"The next night he seated himself in the same position, and begged me to go over the same recital, leaving nothing out. He would question me upon special points to learn how I obtained my faith in God, and the secret of placing myself in the Divine hands. Again, on the third night, he made a similar request, showing the same degree of interest as at first."

On the fourth day the body of Willie was laid away, and Mrs. Pomroy writes of it as follows: "The funeral procession was preceded by twelve pall bearers, wearing a yard of white silk, with long ends tied around their hats, and wreaths of flowers on their arms. Then came the hearse, drawn by two white horses; the President's private carriage, drawn by two black horses; the secretaries and their families, a large number of private carriages, and last of all, the colored help. I never saw anything so imposing."

Little Tad took kindly to his new nurse, and at first would have no one do for him but his father and her; but as he grew better, her desire to see and comfort her sick boys made her anxious to return to them. The President, however, would not dismiss her from his home entirely, but arranged to carry her daily to the hospital. "Tad finally became convalescent," she writes, "and when I left them to go to my poor sick boys, Mrs. Lincoln kissed me and urged Miss Dix to let me come often and see them." A large collection of flowers was cut from the conservatory for her room in the hospital, and Mr. Lincoln accompanied her. During their conversation he told her how much good she had done him, and how encouraged he felt through her ministrations. He said, "When you get to be an old lady, Mrs. Pomroy, tell your grandchildren how indebted the nation was to you in holding up my hands in time of trouble."

Soon after her return she writes the following, under date of March 11th:—

"I am better than when I last wrote, but I have more on my mind than I have ever had since I came to the hospital. We have parted with three of the nurses who would not answer, and another dear nurse by death. She died from fatigue. She was overtaxed, and would not go home to take rest till she was called to her final one. I am doing the work of three nurses. I am placed in charge of the fourth floor, including eighty beds, which is more than I feel able to look after; but there has been so much trouble about the nurses that, God helping me, I will do all that in me lies. . . Yesterday I rode to the Sanitary Commission, in Washington, and from there went to the White House to spend the day.

"Mrs. Lincoln secludes herself from all society, and I was alone with her most of the day in her room. When I told her of my trials and afflictions, and, above all, of God's dealings with me, she could not understand how I could be so happy under it all, and bursting into tears, said she wished she could feel so too. She told the gardener to cut me a bouquet of the richest flowers in the conservatory. At four o'clock the President ordered his horses and open carriage, invited me to ride, and then took me home, to the surprise of all in the hospital. He was not ashamed to be seen riding with the Chelsea nurse, neither was she elated by riding with the President.

"Dear Mrs. F., how mysteriously God works. Two years since, in the seclusion of my little home, I was encouraging my husband to have confidence in God when the time of our separation should come, and now it was given me to tell Mr. Lincoln in my poor, weak way how wonderfully the Lord had sustained me and brought me out of darkness into light. I bade him take courage in this his time of trial, when God was preparing him to stand firm in duty for the salvation of his country. I shall never forget how the tears coursed down his cheeks as I spoke of God's love in affliction, and I besought him to cast his burden upon him. He told me on parting that he enjoyed my visits, to come often, and he would see me home."

In another letter, dated March 27th, she writes as follows: "I was called to go to Washington to get some more clothing for my boys, and I succeeded in securing a large supply of things which was very pleasing to the officers and nurses.

"From the Sanitary Rooms I went to the White House and spent the day. Mrs. Lincoln gave me pictures for my ward, photographs of Willie and Tad, also several dollars' worth of pot plants for my bay window, fruit, and other luxuries for the boys. The President ordered carriage and horses to accompany me to the College."

An incident occurred on their way home which illustrates the homely dignity that accompanied his characteristic kindness of heart. There had been a severe shower the night before, and on going up Fourteenth street the horses became unmanageable, while the carriage got fast in the mud. Mr. Lincoln told the driver to hold one horse, while the footman held the other, till he could get out. He succeeded in finding three large stones, and, with his pantaloons stripped to his knees, and boots covered with mud, he laid the stones down and bore his weight upon them. On coming to the carriage he said, "Now, Mrs. Pomroy, if you will please put your feet just as I tell you, you can reach the sidewalk in safety." Taking hold of her hand, he helped her to the sidewalk, then, looking up, he said, "All through life, be sure and put your feet in the right place, and then *stand firm*." After the carriage was righted, the President looked at his muddy boots in a laughing way, saying, I have always heard of Washington mud, and now I shall take home some as a sample."

It was a well-known fact at that time, that President Lincoln was not connected with any church, and the idea had gained currency that he was an infidel. Happily, these false aspersions have long since given way to a clearer apprehension of the truth, and Mrs. Pomroy has done no little towards righting public opinion. In the confidence of the sick room, bowed under the heavy burden of national calamity and family bereavement, they talked as friend to friend, and the troubled heart would give vent to words not to be misunderstood. Mr. Lincoln was not the man to say things for effect. One day, while leaving the little sufferer in the sick room, to go to his office, he said, "I hope you will pray for him, that he may be spared, if it is God's will; and also for me, for I need the prayers of many."

Again she relates: "When the sad duty came of laying his dear son Willie out of sight, my heart prompted me to say, 'Look up for strength;' and he kindly answered, 'I shall go to God with my sorrows.'" She says, "It was his custom, while waiting for lunch, to take his mother's old worn Bible and lie on the lounge and read. One day he asked me which book I liked to read best, and I told him I was fond of the Psalms. 'Yes,' said he, 'they are the best, for I find in them something for every day in the week. And,' he continued, 'I had a good Christian mother, and her prayers have thus far followed me through.'"

As the officers of the hospital were mostly Catholics, they were bitterly opposed to the holding of any Protestant service, consequently that first prayer meeting was followed by strict orders that it should not be repeated, on penalty of dismissal. While at the White House, Mrs. Pomroy asked and obtained permission to have them continued in her ward, the President remarking, "If there was more praying and less swearing, our country would be safer. We all need to be prayed for, officers as well as privates, and if I were near death, I should like to hear prayer."

While stopping in the President's family, she was waited upon by two young ladies from Washington, who came to volunteer their assistance in organizing and carrying forward a soldiers' prayer meeting in her ward. Shortly after her return to the hospital she writes that a meeting had been held on Sunday afternoon, and that two young ladies assisted, who sang very sweetly to the boys. Among their songs was the "Soldier's Tear," which ever afterwards was a great favorite with them.

These ladies were the Misses Rumsey. Miss Elida, the older sister, in connection with Mr. John A. Fowle, whom she afterwards married, was especially active in promoting the welfare and happiness of the soldiers, visiting them daily, through sunshine and storm, ministering not only to their bodily wants, but supplying food for the intellects and souls of these men who had never been so much in need of it as now.

Stated meetings were held in Mrs. Pomroy's ward, and afterwards in the mess-room, where five or six hundred soldiers would sometimes gather. Here Mr. Fowle often led the meetings, and the Misses Rumsey would electrify their audience with their soul-stirring, patriotic melodies, or melt them to tears with the sweet familiar hymns they used to hear at home. Their philanthropic efforts finally led to a grant of land from the President, in Judiciary Square, upon which they built The Soldiers' Free Library. It grew out of the needs of the army encamped about Washington, and answered its purpose most admirably.

It not only served as library and reading-room, but had accommodations for singing-school and for prayer and conference meetings.

It had articles of membership, the third and last of which read, "I solemnly pledge myself to abstain from profane language, from alcoholic drinks as a beverage, and from all other vices in the army and camp, and will be a true soldier of my country and the cross."

Mr. Fowle was the author of several patriotic songs, among which "The Rebel Flag," set to the tune of "The Sword of Bunker Hill," was always received with the most unbounded admiration by the boys. We insert it on the ground of its intrinsic merit.

THE REBEL FLAG.

Sadly we gazed upon the flag,
    Torn from our brothers' hands,
And shed a tear for those once loved,
    Now joined to traitor bands.
They've put our flag beneath their feet,
    They've trailed it in the dust,
And to the breeze their flag unfurled,
    And placed it in their trust.

Mark what a treacherous deed it was
    From the good old flag to turn,

With us they dwelt beneath its folds,
  But now its stars they spurn.
They've left the flag of Washington,
  The flag our fathers gave;
A richer boon was never given,
  Or prouder flag to wave.

But when the traitors raised their flag
  And marshalled for the fight,
Six hundred thousand freemen rose
  To battle for the right.
Then to our God the prayer went up —
  Protect our noble band;
God blessed our cause, our flag now waves
  Within the traitor's land.

Then down, down, with the rebel flag,
  Tread it beneath your feet,
And gayly to the breeze unfurl,
  That flag we love to greet.
Wave on, ye glorious Stars and Stripes,
  And still our song shall be —
Long live, long live, the good old flag,
  Three cheers, three cheers, for thee!

While singing the last stanza Miss Rumsey would impersonate the defiant spirit of Liberty, by trampling a veritable rebel flag under her feet, at the same time flinging to the breeze the Stars and Stripes. This was always followed by immense cheering and a "tiger" from the boys.

Mrs. Pomroy found in these co-workers such sympathy and assistance that a close bond of friendship was established between them. She became a frequent guest at the home of the Rumseys, when she was not closely confined in the hospital.

In spite of all the sympathy and coöperation received in every department of her work, the fact cannot be lost sight of that she suffered from daily annoyances and trials, some of which grew out of the honorable rank she now took among her associates at the hospital. She writes to a friend at that time, "If you knew all the struggles I am undergoing, you would pity me, I know." Her health was not firm, for her hospital labors at this time were unusually arduous. She writes under date of April 4th, the following:—

"I had to-day a call from the Rev. John Pierpont of Boston, who brought a letter of introduction from Mrs. Lincoln, wishing me to give him a hearing on important business. It was this: Judge S. of Washington, member of the Senate, had a letter sent him from a spirit medium three thousand miles away, requesting him to see Rev. John Pierpont, and ask him to visit a hospital in Washington where there was a widow, who had a husband, son and beautiful daughter in the spirit world, and deliver a message. This message was in the form of a letter, tied with white satin ribbon, which Mr. Pierpont delivered to me. I opened it, and found it purporting to come from my Willie to his mother, in which he says that 'he is happy, and wants her to feel him as always around her; but she heeds him not, and when she is so tired in heart, closing the eyes of those dear ones committed to her care, he wishes to commune with her, and try to ease her mind and make her happy. He has formed the acquaintance of Willie Lincoln in the spirit world, and when his mother was at the White House, the two spirits came and hovered over Willie Lincoln's mother, so that she felt them near, while his mother will take no heed to the spirit influence of her dear son. She often looks at his lock of hair and weeps like a child that will not be comforted.'

"Mr. Pierpont imformed me that this letter was found by Judge S. on his desk, that he delivered it to him to give to me, which he had done on finding me out. Now you can imagine how troubled I was to hear all this and feel obliged to withstand the kind intentions of Mr. Pierpont, whom I then met for the first time, and of Mrs. Lincoln with whom I have had frequent conversations on the subject. He was very earnest in trying to make me feel that this was a direct communication from Willie, and used every argument in his power to convince me of the truth of Spiritualism. But I told him firmly that I could not so see it.

"As we were sitting on the trunks in my little room — for these were the only seats afforded my guests — and I thought on the novelty of the situation, and racked my brain for some form of argument, the key was given me wherewith to unlock the mystery, and I told Mr. Pierpont what I now tell you. Opposite my home in Chelsea, lived Mr. M., a medium, who at the time of my family bereavement used frequently to come in and talk with my husband. He knew all the facts of the case, even to the lock of hair I cut from Willie's curly head. He is now in California, three thousand miles away, and quite likely has a hand in this message. But of course this theory would not satisfy Mr. Pierpont, and he went away disappointed that he could not make a Spiritualist of me. I had the satisfaction, however, of returning his intentional kindness by taking him through the hospital, and, on reaching my ward, he responded to my request, by reading one of his own beautiful poems."

As this grand good type of a Christian gentleman and pastor stood in the centre of an eager group of listeners, his benignant face lighted up with the fires of patriotism, we cannot wonder that he electrified the hearts of his audience, and left only with the promise to come again and repeat the entertainment.

Among the many pleasant friendships formed at the White House was that of Mrs. Secretary Wells. She called daily during the sickness of little Tad, and was always very cordial in her manner towards Mrs. Pomroy. Both had sons on the battle-field, were interested in the work of ameliorating suffering, and when she returned to the hospital, Mrs. Wells and her husband proved unfailing friends. One August afternoon she called on Mrs. Pomroy. The thermometer ranged from ninety to one hundred, and the air of the sick room was stifling in the extreme.

The poor sufferers tossed from side to side, restless with fever heat, or lay on their cots, passive with weakness. Mrs. Wells, with ready sympathy, divined the needs of the sick men, and said to the nurse, "I have ice cream in the cellar, at home, and as soon as I get there I shall send you up ten quarts for your boys." Delighted with her secret, for this was to be a surprise to them, Mrs. Pomroy waited impatiently for the return of Mrs. Wells' carriage, which after a time made its appearance.

The footman alighted with his freight, and was immediately met by the steward, who ordered it to be sent to his department.

The man remonstrated, saying it was for Mrs. Pomroy's sickest men; but the steward was imperative. Mrs. Pomroy, observing the course of things from her upper window, well knowing that if it reached the officers' rooms the boys would not receive the smallest amount, took the matter in hand by going down, claiming the delicacy as a gift from Mrs. Wells, and declaring that the boys should have every particle of it. She carried the day. Her boys were delighted with their mug of ice cream; then every other ward in the hospital was visited, and the sickest boys in each had their portion. The blessings rained down upon her by those grateful men were such as she will never forget.

Not long afterward a large box containing jellies, wines, tea, coffee, slings and the like was sent to her from Salem. On its arrival, the steward ordered it into his office, had the contents taken out and arranged on his shelves, designing them for his private use, and had the box split up for kindlings. One of Mrs. Pomroy's boys, on going to the shed, saw the remnants of the demolished box, with her name stamped upon it, and immediately informed her. She at once appealed to the surgeon in charge, who ordered an investigation, whereupon the bottles and jars marked for Mrs. Pomroy's private use were found in the possession of the steward. He was obliged to give them into her care and ordered not to repeat the theft again. We infer from what follows that Mrs. Pomroy never stood high in favor with the steward after this.

At this time the soldiers were suffering for the want of supplies. Great scarcity induced high prices. Milk was twenty-five cents a quart; eggs seventy-five cents a dozen, butter correspondingly high, and of such a quality as called forth the remark from one of the men that "he had heard of rank butter, but this butter outranked General Grant himself." The bread was so poor and hard that frequently the men refused to eat it. It was Mrs. Pomroy's habit to go round and gather up the pieces of bread that remained on their plates, keep them until enough had been gained for a pudding, then, out of her own means, she would buy milk, sugar and other necessary ingredients, and make them a pudding, sending it down to the bakery, to be cooked. The boys had come to look forward to their pudding as a treat; but the steward, on finding the matter out, put an immediate stop to the "extravagance of that Massachusetts nurse."

The Soldier's Union Relief Association did much towards ameliorating the condition of the poor soldiers, exposing as it did the fraudulent methods practised upon them by designing officers. A visiting commitee was sent into the hospitals to inquire into and report on the amount and quality of the supplies furnished. Their report as to tea and coffee supplied to Columbia College was, "the same miserable, unwholesome trash furnished to nearly all the hospitals: trash unfit to drench the meanest brute. Some of the surgeons expressed aversion to good living, lest the soldier become wedded to hospital life."

When the men grew so tired of this drink they could not taste it, Mrs. Pomroy would sometimes go down into the nurse's kitchen, fill the teakettle there, and sending down for a pitcher of the boiling water, would prepare a good, "old-fashioned cup of Northern tea," as the boys called it. The steward, however, found it out, and forbade her having another drop of hot water.

That same day Secretary Wells called on her, to ask if there was anything she wanted, for, said he, "President Lincoln declares that Mrs. Pomroy shall have everything she wants." She thereupon told him of her unsuccessful attempt at providing tea. "Well, Mrs. Pomroy," he said, "bear it patiently, it will all come out right in the end. You have borne a good deal, but you deserve everything you want, and shall have it if I can get it for you."

As a result of this, an oil stove, with all needful appurtenances, was sent immediately to her, and the boys triumphantly mounted it on a shelf in a convenient part of the bath-room. Then and there was inaugurated a fragrant cup of tea, first of the many that followed to the end of her stay in the hospital. The next day the steward came up at a time when the odor of boiling hot tea, such as was not common in the other hospital wards, caused him to look around and inquire, "What does this mean?" The nurse directed his attention to the bath-room, whence the odor proceeded, and he perceived, to his astonishment, the oil stove in full operation. Mrs. Pomroy explained that it was a gift from Secretary Wells, and the discomfitted officer left without further observation.

In a letter written during the month of April, she speaks of a young lady who visited the hospital and charmed the boys by her sweet singing. This was none other than the notable Miss Gilson, from Chelsea, known as one of the soldiers' best friends. She was at this time about commencing her labor of love, not the least part of which was the service of song which she so admirably rendered. Among the familiar home melodies that melted them to tears or roused their military ardor, were "Do they miss me at Home?" "Who will care for Mother now?" and the "Star Spangled Banner." During Mrs. Pomroy's first furlough, Miss Gilson took her place as substitute, after which she went out to the more arduous duties of the battle-field.

> There is no holy service
> But hath its secret bliss;
> Yet of all blessed ministries,
> Is one so dear as this?

CHAPTER IV.

ALL MY SPRINGS ARE IN THEE.

THROUGH all the trying scenes of the winter and spring of this, her first year of hospital life, strange as it may seem, Mrs. Pomroy's health improved. Physical strength suited to every emergency was vouchsafed to her, and she was a wonder to herself and to friends who had prophesied her speedy return home, from over-exhaustion.

At the approach of warm weather, however, her system was in the condition to take in the malaria, which taints the air of that region more or less at all seasons, and she had an attack of chills and fever that somewhat reduced her health and spirits. It came under Mr. Lincoln's notice during one of her calls at the Presidential mansion, and he arranged with Miss Dix for her to have a short furlough, to be spent in his family. During her visit she writes as follows:

"I am having a furlough, and what seems so very singular, I was thinking whether I had better get one for two or three days — for I needed the rest and felt as though I was growing old fast — when I heard that Miss Dix had said she gave no furloughs to any of her nurses, and if they chose to go away, they must stay away altogether.

"But a note was sent to Miss Dix from the President, requesting her to let me come and keep Mrs. Lincoln company, as Mrs. Edwards, her sister, was called suddenly home to Illinois. Miss Dix, of course, granted his request, and, for fear I might lose my pleasant ward in the hospital, the President wrote to the surgeon in charge, requesting him to reserve my place for me, when I should return. So here I am, safe under his protection.

"Mrs. Lincoln is very anxious for me to stay here all summer; but if I cannot, always to come here for rest. Everything is done for my comfort, and I. go to ride with them every day. . . . . I am living three years in one, but I am jogging on in my usual steady way, taking that good, old-fashioned book as my guide and comfort. Mrs. Lincoln needs the comfort of it, too. She says she is tired of being a slave to the world, and 'would live on bread and water if she could feel as happy as I do.'

"We have frequent conversations on these things, and my heart yearns to see her seeking comfort in something besides these unstable pleasures." She writes to a friend later on:

"I heard yesterday that two hundred and fifty wounded soldiers were to be sent to Columbia to-day, and it seems as though I could not stay away from them any longer. . . . . I have so many calls for little sums of money among the sick, that I have spent much of my own means to help them along. I buy them little luxuries which they really need, and when they want their own clothing washed, I often pay for it, as the hospital clothing is all that is washed free of expense. They often go to their regiments forgetting to pay me, but I do not care for that, only I do wish so much, at times, that I was possessed of more means. Then there are some soldiers' families just back of the hospital. The husbands are far away, and they are in almost a starving condition, and I can buy milk and bread for them as long as I have anything to buy with. I never stop to ask, Who is my neighbor? in times of sickness or distress.

"General ——'s wife had a serenade last evening, and she came out on the piazza with her babe wrapped in the flag of our country. What a patriotic woman! She is like many another here, who cannot look upon a poor wounded soldier, nor give anything, except to men in office. They are nothing to them if they are privates.

"Another general's wife says she wonders how I can be with soldiers in a hospital. I told her if she were there a week, she would have a good appetite and sleep all night just as I do, for I happened to know that she had no appetite, and slept very little. . . . The President and Mrs. Lincoln still continue to urge me to stay with them this summer, but no temptation, only a sense of duty, would prompt me to remain away from my boys. I try to enjoy all I can while here, but I did not realize what my Heavenly Father had in store, to try me and make me cling closer to him, as daily new and untried experiences and temptations come to me. But my confidence is strong thus far that he has led me on, and I trust him for the future.''

The wounded men to whom she refers as being brought to the hospital, were doubtless from the field of Williamsburg, where the brave Hentzleman and his men brought the rebels to bay in their flight from Yorktown. Rooted to the bloody field, they withstood the assaults of the enemy till help came, though every third man had fallen. The loss in numbers was heavy, but the indomitable persistence of both officers and men gained the victory, and a thrill of confidence in Northern leadership again pulsated through the land. Events seemed to promise a termination of the war, as the lines of the two great armies drew closer together in different sections of the country.

In Congress the question of emancipating the slaves was claiming a large share of attention. Already a considerable number in both Houses insisted that a decree of universal emancipation was necessary to put down the rebellion, while others claimed that it was an act of injustice to the South. The act of emancipation in the District of Columbia had been passed, signed by the President, and become a law, but that did not satisfy the people.

Every one felt the peril of the hour, but none felt the burden of it like our beloved President. Nothing kept him from sinking wholly underneath the load of calumny and weighty cares that beset him day and night, but the strong will of the man combined with his wonderful facility in extracting comfort out of the pleasant trivialities of every-day life. Even his little dog Jip was instrumental in relieving his master of some portion of the burden, for the little fellow was never absent from the Presidential lunch. He was always in Mr. Lincoln's lap to claim his portion first, and was caressed and petted by him through the whole meal.

Often he would come in haggard and weary, sinking into the chair almost helpless, and would cast about on the shelf near at hand, for a book containing Dame Partington's sayings, and in some trivial bit of humor, which he would read to Mrs. Pomroy, laugh away the cloud of weariness that had settled upon him.

Sometimes it was Shakespeare, of which he had a most profound appreciation, often reading aloud, in beautifully modulated accents, the thoughts that charmed him most. Then it would be the old family Bible of his mother's, persuading him with an eloquence beyond that of words, to hold on through the struggle, as she, poor woman, had done, till victory should come.

Often the strain upon brain and body was relaxed by living over boyhood's days — rehearsing events through which he had passed. He said to Mrs. Pomroy at one time, "Did I ever tell you about my first dollar? I prized that more than five now, and, for once in my life, I felt rich. I was eighteen years old, quite a tall boy, and belonged to a class they called *scrubs* — people who did not own slaves, but had to work very hard to raise their own produce and then take it down the river to sell.

"After getting my mother's consent (for I always went to her for advice), I constructed a little flat-boat, large enough to take a barrel, with other things, down to New Orleans. A steamer was coming down the river. There were no wharves then, and passengers had to go out in small boats to the steamer. While passing down the river, two men accosted me with, 'Who owns that boat?' I answered, 'I do.'

"'Will you,' said they, 'take our trunks to the steamer?'

"'Certainly,' I said, and their trunks were put on board. They seated themselves upon them, and then each threw a silver half-dollar on the floor of my boat. As I picked them up, I never felt so happy or so rich in my life, to think I was the owner of a dollar."

One day when Tad was looking at some picture-books that a friend had sent him, the President remarked, "How many books there are for children nowadays. When I was a boy, I learned my letters by the blaze of a pitchpine knot, laying myself down flat, and my now sainted mother teaching me the large

MR. LINCOLN AND "TAD." (*Page* 85.)

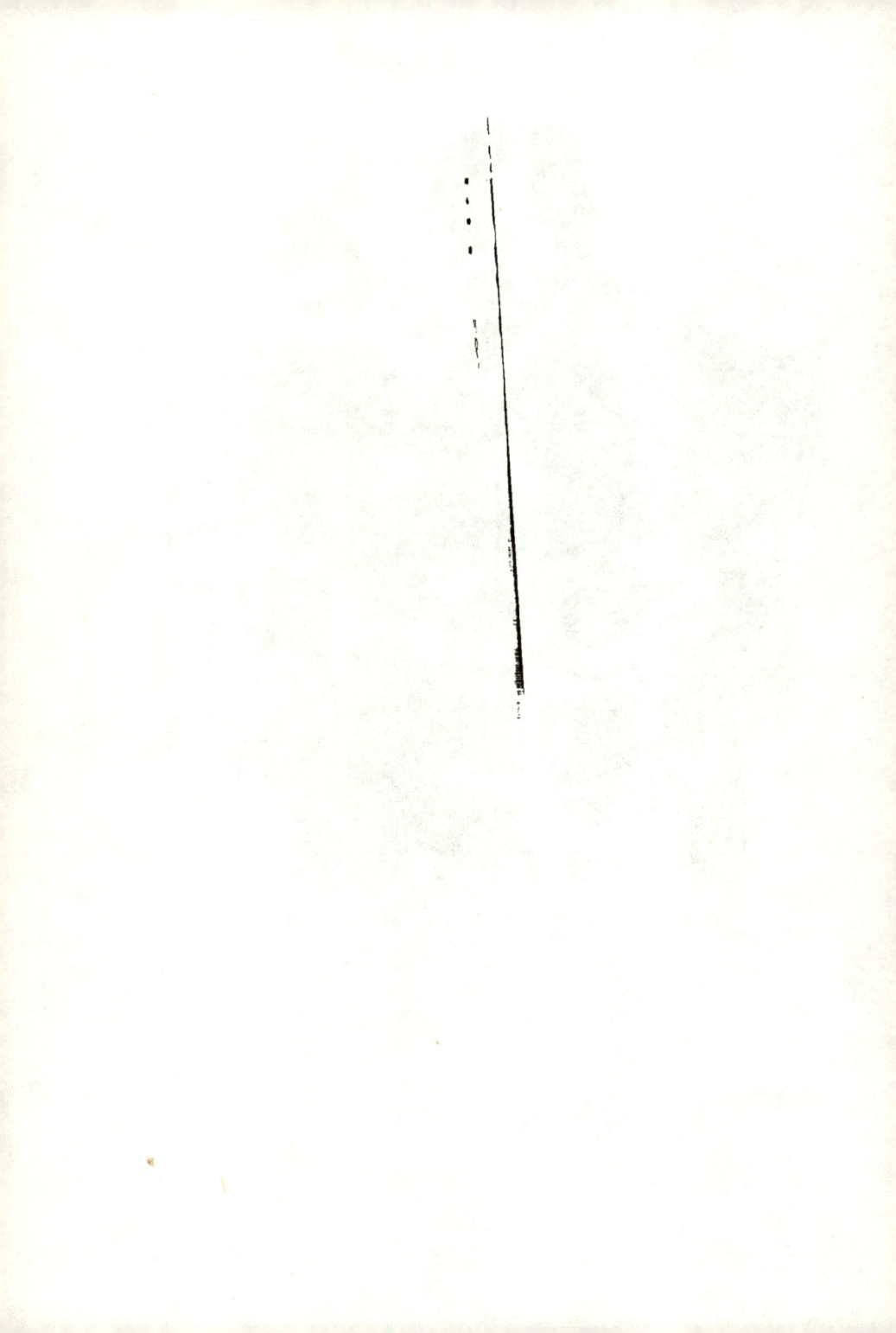

letters from her Bible. She was all the teacher I had in those times, and often when pressed with letters I think of her, as she instructed me how to hold the pen, telling me if I lived to be a man I might find some writing to do."

Little Tad furnished another bright spot of comfort for the President. He took great delight in the child's infinite fund of boisterous mirth and mischievous pranks. After his brother Willie's death and the departure of Robert for college, he was idolized and petted by father and mother, by teachers and visitors, till he became the most absolute little monarch ever known at the White House. He had a very poor opinion of books, and of teachers, if they attempted discipline, or interfered in any way with his cherished schemes, and in that case he was shrewd enough to get rid of them.

."Let him run," said the President; "he will have time enough to learn his letters and get poky." From early in the morning till late at night he kept the house alive with his fantastic pranks; yoking his kids to chairs, drawing his dogs tandem over the lawn, and even taking the affairs of state in hand, in which he showed a degree of discernment and appreciation of merit beyond that of many an older head, for he would treat flatterers and office seekers with a curious coolness and contempt, but often would espouse the cause of some poor widow or tattered soldier, whom he found waiting in the ante-rooms, dragging them into the executive presence, ordering the ushers out of the way and demanding immediate action from headquarters. The President rarely denied a hearing, no matter how closely pressed in other directions.

One day the little fellow had a present of a box of tools from some friend, out of which grew a fund of exciting occupation, both for himself and the inmates of the mansion. The new saw was tested by cutting away the plank leading from the dining-room to the conservatory, knobs and locks were taken off the doors, and nails driven into the floor through elegant carpets. It was only Mrs. Pomroy's appeal to Mr. Lincoln, and his threat of taking the tools away from his little son, that saved the mansion from further detruction.

It was during this period of her sojourn here that a celebrated artist was engaged on a full length picture of Mr. Lincoln. Every morning the ladies were called down to give their opinion on the work in progress.

One morning great consternation prevailed. The young sprite of the household had locked the door upon the artist at his work, and taken himself off with the key. Servants were despatched in every direction for the young miscreant, who was laughing in his sleeves at the breeze he had created, and did not return till some hours afterward, during which time another key had been provided to let out the imprisoned artist. During this visit Mrs. Pomroy spent her nights in the Presidential guest chamber, and relates an incident in substance as follows:

"I passed along the dreary corridors behind poor aunt Mary, who had offered to wait upon me in any capacity, and who left me at the door, kissing my hands, with a 'God bress ye, honey!' The stately grandeur of my surroundings, contrasting so vividly with my previous hospital accommodations, together with the gaslight always kept up in each room, prevented my sleep till a late hour. When I did awake I saw an apparition at my open door that made my hair stand on end. By the dim light, I could just discern a burly figure, surmounted by a woolly head and a grinning row of ivories, with a long cudgel, as it seemed to me, in his uplifted hand. I could just find breath to gasp 'What do you want?' when the well-known voice of Sambo reassured me, saying, 'I's only the fireman; don't be afraid, missis.' Whereupon I subsided, while he came forward and replenished my coal grate, the long cudgel taking the proportions of a poker, which was vigorously applied thereto. This practice was a customary event of each night, and never afterwards disturbed the quiet of my slumbers."

Her three weeks' furlough at the White House passed rapidly, and she returned to her boys with renewed strength and interest. She writes shortly after the battle of Winchester: "I can assure you we are seeing trouble sometimes. Two hundred and fifty came to us last week, and last night, just at dark, we had sixty poor, wounded, discouraged soldiers, so worn out that as they came up the stairs it seemed as though they would faint away. I cannot describe my feelings when told to arrange my beds for more wounded men, and let those who are getting better sleep on the floor, if there was no other place for them.

"After they were conducted to the bath room and washed, and had clean clothes, I took them by the hand and told them they had come to a good place, and I would do all for them I could. You never saw such gratitude. They had not heard a kind, womanly word since they left home; and then the tears! O, Mrs. F., were you here, your heart would ache, for seeing and assisting to dress the wounds, is very different form hearing about it a long way off. My hands and head and heart are full; for I have never seen anything like this before. . . . I have singing and prayer meetings now, every Sabbath; and for the last two Sabbaths have had a Bible class, and fourteen of my boys are studying the Bible. Every morning I take time to read a chapter to them, and am surprised to see what attention they give.

"We have long needed a chaplain; all the nurses feel interested to have one, and many of the soldiers. I spoke to the President about it, and after hearing what I had to say, he told me I had better petition. I wrote a letter, which was read before the Senate, and the President came last night to tell me that he thought my desires would be gratified, as he should do his best to get the Rev. Mr. D. the chaplaincy for Columbia College. And still further; he is going to give my son George a lieutenancy in the regular army. . . . . . Our tents and barracks back of the hospital are full of the wounded, and if any societies in the towns around Boston would like to help, *now* is the time, as the wounded are coming upon us so fast that shirts and drawers, cotton socks, coarse combs, small pins, handkerchiefs and old linen, and some of the luxuries that we cannot get here, will be very acceptable.

"How I do dislike to beg; but I am spending daily my own money for these things. They are grateful for the *smallest favors*. . . . I suppose you have heard of the death of two of Miss Dix's nurses. They were in a Southern hospital doing God and their country service, and she left them happy as she left us. Soon after the hospital was attacked by rebel soldiery, two were killed outright, and the other eight fled, it is supposed, and are still missing. How sad! and yet, some of us in Washington may share the same fate. We are surrounded by Secesh, and they are only waiting their time.

"We have been having trouble here with the nurses; two have been expelled. Miss Dix talks of removing some of the best to Fortress Monroe, which is a hard place for any one to go to; but I wait patiently, trusting my Heavenly Father. Mrs. Lincoln is very anxious that I should leave the hospital and make my home with her, but I do not know what a day may bring forth, and I do not encourage her in the least. I am happy here in doing my duty by these brave men, and would not change places with Mrs. Lincoln for all her honors. She suffers from depression of spirits, but I do think if she would only come here and look at the poor soldiers occasionally it would be better for her. . . . Let my name be kept as quiet as possible, for I am surprised to find it so much handled. I have clergymen, superintendents, and quite distinguished gentlemen, inquire for my name at the office, and my time has been very much taken up in citing peculiar cases that have come under my observation. One gentleman from the far West has offered pay if I will write to him for his Sunday-school paper. Of course I cannot."

When we take into account that nearly all her letters to friends were written at night, after the laborious duties of the day had been performed, often taken up in the hours of the midnight watch with the dying, to keep herself from falling asleep, we cannot wonder that she had no disposition to gratify the world of inquirers through the agency of letters.

She writes, later on: "It is just nine months to-day since I set foot into this place of suffering, and I have no desire to return home while I can make myself useful. I do not know any one with whom I would exchange situations; for in spite of the rudeness of his surroundings, there is a charm that invests the poor soldier boy. When once you have enlisted his affection, he makes a confident of you, and before you are aware of it, you are mother, nurse and friend. Then he will listen to reproof and instruction.

"I have a little Vermont fellow for an attendant, for whom I feel responsible to God. He is an orphan boy, and loves me dearly. He says I am the only mother he ever knew. He shares with me all my presents, and when, the other day, I gave him a piece of pie, he did not speak for the tears that choked him. He says I am too good to him. He had been cruelly treated before coming here, and is all the more susceptible to kindly influences now. God grant me help to reach his inner feelings, so as to instruct him in becoming a good Christian boy."

During one of Mrs. Pomroy's visits to the White House, Mr. Lincoln said to her, "Mrs. Pomroy, I want to do something for you; what shall it be? Be perfectly free to tell me what you want most, and if it is in my power, you shall have it."

Taken unawares by this generous proffer, she knew not what to reply. She knew no want uppermost for herself, so entirely was she leaning from day to day upon Divine favor, in her new, strange life.

It finally came to her in this way: "If Mr. Lincoln would only come to Columbia College and see my boys, how much good it would do them!" And so, the next day, she proffered her simple request.

The promise was granted with apparent pleasure and attended to with alacrity; for within a week, the Presidential carriage was drawn up at Columbia College, and the President, and Senator Browning, from Illinois, alighted, and called for Mrs. Pomroy. She writes in a letter that follows:

"I was in my room at the time, and the surgeon in charge came and told me that the President would like to see me. As I went to the door, lo and behold! a great company of gentlemen were waiting for me to introduce them to His Excellency. I was taken by surprise and did the honors of introducing him to all the surgeons, stewards, cadets, and the gentlemen that followed, as well as the nurses. Then the Surgeon-General invited me to do escort duty to the President, by going all through the hospital, which I did, and then went out into the tents and performed the duty there. The soldiers were called out by the officers, arranged in a straight line, and Mr. Lincoln, in his unpretentious way, with his hat off, shook hands with each one, asking his name and the name of his regiment and company. Such a scene will never be effaced from the memory of the soldiers as the lame, halt and withered came straggling into line at the unexpected beat of the drum.

"Their enthusiasm was unbounded, and they expressed their minds after the interview by saying, 'We'll vote him in next election.'

"One poor fellow for days afterwards refused to wash the hand that had grasped the President's."

The pleasantest and most uncommon scene of the event was where Mrs. Pomroy sent down into the kitchen and cook-room and ordered colored Lucy and the two male colored servants to wash their hands and make ready to come up. They stood on either side of her as the President passed out. "And who are these?" he said, in a kindly tone.

"This is Lucy, formerly a slave from Kentucky. She cooks the nurses' food."

"How do you do, Lucy?" and out went that long hand in recognition of the woman's services.

"And who are these on your left?"

"This is Garner, and this Brown. They are serving their country by cooking the low diet for our sickest boys."

Then again the hearty grip, with "How do you do, Garner? how do you do, Brown?" their shining faces meanwhile attesting their amazement and joy for all time, thus to be addressed by their beloved President.

Mrs. Pomroy escorted him to the outer entrance, and the carriage drove away; but no sooner was it lost to view than she became aware of a feeling of intense disapprobation and disgust among the officers, who a moment before had been all graciousness and suavity.

Their conversation was afterwards reported to her. "Anybody would know she was a Massachusetts woman," they said, "for no one else would do such a mean, contemptible trick as to introduce those d—— niggers to the President."

"Yes," said the surgeon in charge, "it was in Massachusetts that the first *abolition egg* was laid."

Even the soldiers imbibed the spirit of their superiors, and felt their honor insulted.

Mrs. Pomroy's attendant came to her shortly after and said, "Mother, what could you be thinking of to introduce those niggers to the President?" "Charlie," she said, "who maketh thee to differ? Does God think the less of these poor people because their skin is black?" Her earnest and fearless appeal in behalf of these poor, despised creatures did much towards restoring harmony, and she was loaded with thanks for the pleasure she had conferred upon officers and soldiers for a week succeeding; but the colored help never ceased to attest their gratitude. "Lub ye, Missus, long as ye lib. Nebber spec such a t'ing!"

Shortly after, the carriage was sent from the White House to bring Mrs. Pomroy for a visit. Having a good opportunity, she asked the President if his feelings were hurt on being presented to the colored servants of Columbia College. "Hurt? No, indeed!" he said; "it did my soul good. I'm glad to do them honor. It will not be long before we shall have to use them as soldiers and call them into the ranks side by side with their white brothers."

Among her patients at this time was a young Frenchman, Charlemagne by name. He was a member of a New York regiment, and had been brought in with a bad leg-wound.

He was unable to speak a word of English, and would lie watching every motion of his nurse, with an expression of patience on his beautiful countenance that was very pathetic, even to the most casual observer. No one in the hospital was able to converse with him, and the happy expedient of calling in Robert Lincoln, who was then home from college, was resorted to.

It was a very sorry thing for this voluble

and accomplished young Frenchman to forego the exercise of his vocal powers, and his delight was unbounded when he found a young companion to converse with. Robert would come in quite often to talk and read to him, bringing papers, fruit and delicacies.

When it was thought necessary by his physicians that his leg should be amputated, the poor fellow shook his head, and Robert had to be called in to explain that he could not live unless it were done, and that the operation would not be so trying as he expected. He finally consented, if "Mudder would stay by him."

This his nurse consented to do. She went with him into the operating room, administered the chloroform and assisted the surgeon during the process of amputation. Charlemagne was raised up from his bed of sickness, and at the end of six months hobbled down to Washington on crutches, for his new leg.

Shortly afterwards he stepped into the hospital and presented himself to his nurse, exclaiming in triumph, as he put his feet together, "Which one is it, mudder?" So neat a piece of workmanship was presented to her admiring gaze, that she was forced to confess, much to his delight, that she could not tell which.

So much coolness and courage was shown by Mrs. Pomroy in the operating-room, that she was frequently called on to assist the surgeons, and in dressing wounds she was considered quite an adept. Her basket containing lint, bandages and scissors, was in frequent requisition, and the pale, frail-looking nurse was acknowledged to have the steadiest hand of them all.

At one time, fifteen men were brought in whose left legs required amputation. Morning and evening, for the space of three months, she held the shattered stumps while the surgeon dressed and bandaged them.

One peculiarly trying case was that of Skennel, of Maine. He was brought in from the battle-field with an ugly wound in the leg, resulting from having his horse shot under him. He had complained for several hours of a crawling and biting sensation in his wound, which gave him so much uneasiness and pain that he could get no rest. The young surgeon who attended him, anticipating an evening of gayety in Washington, and anxious to leave for the night, declared there was no help for it, and that he would do nothing more for him, leaving him in care of his nurse.

The poor fellow's limb was confined firmly in a wooden box, where he had no means of moving it. The biting and crawling feeling still continued, and the nurse filled with sympathy for his distress, determined, with the help of her assistant, to unstrap the limb and examine the wound. As she did so, a sickening sight was brought to view; for it was literally alive with vermin which had bred there, through some insect germ in the cotton, it was supposed.

With her attendant's aid Mrs. Pomroy washed and dressed the wound and put it back into place, as she had seen the surgeon do. This accomplished, the poor soldier's eyes shone with relief and gratitude, then closed in peaceful slumber for the remainder of the night, while his weary nurse rested also, with the consciousness of another day's work completed.

Her own simple version of some of these

trying incidents will prove what an unfailing support her courage and sympathy was in the soldiers' hour of deepest distress.

In a letter written during the month of August, she says: "I dressed two of my boys in a clean outfit for the operating room, after fixing the table, getting sponges, basins, oil cloth and tub; then took one of them by the hand and led him into the room, assisted him on to the operating-table, and kept hold of his hand till all was through. Oh, how grateful was that dear young man! He was then put in bed, and my older boy, a Massachusetts man, forty-two years old, was then called, and I did the same by him.

"How little the wives and mothers at home know what their dear ones are passing through! Tears, yes, tears of gratitude do I witness from stout-hearted men, when I go to them and say, 'Good courage, friend! we will do all we can for you.'

"The week before I had a young man wounded in the ankle, and after all my care for nine weeks, it was decided that the foot must be amputated. His agony at the thought of going home to his mother with only one foot, was hard to witness. At length he consented to the operation, if I would take hold of his hand, which I did, and when all was through, he kissed me like an own child, saying, 'You are a good mother to me.' My journal! how that will tell the tale when I am laid away and cannot voice the scenes that thrill me through, and will continue to, while life and memory last."

Again she writes: "We have had one rebel brought to our care, who died with fever. Until his last breath, he swore vengeance upon us. The doctors had no patience with him. A post-mortem examination was made, and I need not tell the rest, for one of the surgeons informed me privately, that if he could do no good for his country, his body should be of use to scientific men.

"It seems to me we have more Secessionists in Washington than people have any idea. My visits to the White House have opened my eyes. The city is filled with military officers who daily visit our select aristocracy, loitering on the steps of public buildings, and mingling in the vilest society, while our poor Northern privates have to bear the burden and heat of the day. Our fields are scattered with the wounded and dying, and the President tells me he thinks this will be a long war yet. We live in exciting times at the hospital. Our old faithful attendants have been taken from us, and we are now dependent on poor sick convalescents, who can hardly carry themselves about, much more do any work. Also a new set of surgeons, who are putting on the screws tighter than ever; and what with our beds full, and the many hospital trials, we nurses ought to have the patience of Job, the wisdom of a Solomon, and the spirit of Peter, when he cried out, 'Lord, save, or we perish.' Do not think I am homesick or worn out. Oh, no! far from that; but military rules are so strict, and the Stripes use so much authority, that we all get tired, sometimes; but so long as my health is good, just so long shall I stand by the poor private who risks his life for our country. If I come down to bread alone, it will not trouble me in the least, for as long as I have a little money by me, I can surely take care of myself.

"On Tuesday last I had a pleasant ride with some Washington friends. We went first to the Soldiers' Home, a place owned by government, centaining three hundred acres, on which are five stone houses, and a larger one for the aged and crippled soldiers who have fought their country's battles, and have settled down quietly till the Great Captain calls them up higher. We rode round the President's country seat, which is one of the five houses, and from there to the graveyard; and a more sorrowful sight I have never seen.

"There lay our soldiers, over eighteen hundred of them, with only a footpath between them; and as I wandered through, to look after my twenty-four boys who had been laid there, I would occasionally read on the wooden slab, '*Name unknown.*' I could help contrasting that sad and lonely place — not a tree or flower could be seen — to that of our beautiful Woodlawn, with its clinging vines, ornamental shrubbery, and costly monuments. The tears would come when I thought of the poor soldiers borne here now, not by the drum and fife, but only by the chaplain, who walks by the side of the cart, shedding tears of sympathy for those at home. Such is war time, and the end is not yet."

Again she writes: "We are all excitement, as the report is that our most trusted leaders have skedaddled, and fears are entertained that the rebels will get possession of Washington. What does all this mean? Our soldiers are tired of the war; thousands are dying, and who will fill their places? Do we not live in trying times?"

>   Turn and o'erturn, Outstretched Hand,
>   Nor stint nor stay;
>   The years have never dropped their sand
>   On mortal issues half so grand
>   As ours to day.

CHAPTER V.

LED ON.

THE excitement and suspicion with regard to the condition of our army, to which Mrs. Pomroy refers, were not without warrant. General Pope's campaign had proved a failure.

The people instead of celebrating the Fourth of July in the overthrow of Richmond, as they had anticipated, were forced to see our army retreat and the enemy advance in their rear, with the evident intention of moving boldly upon Washington. The hospitals in and around that city were rapidly filling up with the wounded and dying heroes of the Army of the Potomac, and additional tents were supplied.

Surgeons and experienced physicians came flocking in from the different States, and not only Washington, but the whole North, was alarmed.

Already General Lee was throwing his army across the Potomac; clouds of ominous smoke were gathering in the distance, and the sound of heavy cannonading could be heard ten miles away. At this perilous time Mrs. Pomroy visited a section of country near which the enemy was encamped. We give a description of it in her own words:

"A few days since my friends who are interested in the soldiers at the hospitals, and are favored with an ambulance daily, came for me to go to Falls Church, in Virginia, and the change was a pleasant one. After going through part of Georgetown, we crossed the Canal Bridge, which was built to carry our troops over to the Virginia side.

"While passing along there was presented such a scene of desolation—trees felled on both sides of the road for our troops to pitch their tents, and for several miles scarcely a house till we arrived at Falls Church. The first place we stopped at was the Guard House, to procure a pass, and we were told to be home before dark, as the Guerrillas were back of the woods and might fire upon us. The caution was not unnecessary, for I learned through Mr. Fowle afterwards, that they were out on a raid that night, and not far from us when we re-crossed the bridge.

"We stopped at the house that Stonewall Jackson had kept for his headquarters, and from thence went to Fort Corcoran. Then we recollected hearing our boys tell of working sixty days to get that grand and beautiful piece of workmanship accomplished. It was well mounted with cannon whose mouths could send forth balls to a distance of several miles.

"The next place visited was a hospital for the sick, which was formerly a Baptist church, but now our sick are taken in and kindly cared for. There were sixty poor fellows; and as we gave them shirts, sheets, wines, papers, tracts and Bibles, I cannot tell you the number of happy faces we left.

"A few rods further we came to Falls Church, a small, neat, brick building, one story and a half high. Here the enemy stopped until they were driven back; and after the skirmish that ensued, the rebels that were killed were laid side by side with the Union men. Half a mile from here we went on a hill named Cameron Encampment, which was covered with tents; and here sixteen hundred poor fellows, disabled from the skirmish, were brought. As we passed from tent to tent, and saw so many of our dear boys, some too sick to speak, while others hobbled along on crutches and sticks, others with arms, limbs and heads bound up, my heart cried out, 'How long O, Lord, how long!'

"On the top of the hill was a flag-staff, and a flag was thrown to the breeze. Mr. Fowle had the drum beat, for the boys to rally round the flag, which they did with alacrity, giving it three rousing cheers. Then Miss Rumsey, the sweet singer of Washington, sang the *Star Spangled Banner*, and the *Rebel Flag*, and all the boys were invited to join in the chorus, and if they could not sing, to open their mouths, which they did to the gratification of all there, while they sang *Rally round the Flag;* a circle composed of nearly five hundred gathered about the flag staff, as they formed in three or four rows, some sitting, others standing.

"I had the pleasure of distributing tracts, papers and Bibles to them while my young friend continued to sing. Last of all, we sang *America*, and we broke away after immense cheering for old Massachusetts. We then shook hands with the surgeons, and they heartily urged us to come again, and let our friends at the North know that their kindness was appreciated.

"On Saturday the battle was going on, and every one that could procure a horse went to the field to look after our wounded, and on Saturday night the wounded thronged our streets, as carriages, omnibuses and ambulances were engaged in bringing them from the field. On Sunday we let all our convalescents go to other hospitals, and we filled up with wounded. An order came from Washington to prepare for eight thousand."

The next letter she writes is descriptive of the event of this influx of suffering men:

"On the Sabbath, at four o'clock in the morning, three hundred were brought in from the battle-field, and all the nurses, stewards, physicians and cooks were called up to look after them. Several were so completely exhausted that they died while being taken out of the ambulances. We are so full that our entries, and every spare place, are covered with beds, and our poor boys are lying so thick that we have to be careful how and where we step. Such horrid sights I cannot describe. Men with both eyes put out, others with arms hanging as the ball went through them, others with legs shot off or hanging helpless. They seemed like children waiting for their mothers' care.

"As we stepped among them as carefully as we could, it was enough to make the stoutest heart faint to witness the ghastly wounds, and hear their pathetic appeals — 'Do take me from here!' 'Please give me a drink of water!' 'I'm so faint!' 'O God, but I'm in so much pain!' 'If my mother were here, she would not let me die so.'

"We supplied them first of all with water, tea, coffee or stimulants, then, as fast as we could, we washed and dressed their wounds, cut and combed their hair. Then in clean clothes, when quietly in bed, how the manly tears would start as they thought of wife and mother.

"O, Mrs. F., think of the old gray-haired man with his locks saturated with blood from a wound in the head; then a stout man of forty with his hip so mangled that when I assist them in taking care of him, the big tears roll off and he blesses me and calls me God's angel; and still another having a ball cut through his ankle, and I helping the surgeon, by holding the leg, as we cannot spare time to give chloroform. O these sights and scenes; how they burn themselves into my brain!

"We have to-day eight hundred wounded, and I am the only female nurse on the fourth ward, as Miss Dix has taken my mate to the battle-field with her. She would have taken me also, had I been strong enough to bear the fatigue.

"I have now ninety-one beds to look after, but the dear Lord is helping me to do whatever is laid upon me. Truly I can say from the fulness of my heart, His mercies are 'new every morning and fresh every evening.'

"There is no Sunday here. All is confusion and excitement, and the two last Sabbaths I shall never forget; no, never! We have no time to stop and think, but our judgment regarding what is to be done, must be in our fingers' ends, so to speak, as we have to act speedily or lose it entirely.

"My son George is now under my care, as he came in completely fatigued and worn out. He was ordered to New York, with one hundred others, and the conductor having heard of me, procured him a passage for Washington. He was then sent to Armory Hospital, and my surgeon in charge got a transfer to this place. He is doing well; has been in four battles, and the Lord spared him, while companions fell dead at his side."

October 2d she writes as follows: "I am expecting to-day to go home with Mrs. Lincoln and spend a few days, as I am completely worn down with fatigue, and feel sometimes like Martha, 'careful and troubled about many things.' All my time has been spent in working or writing. There is no end to the letters I have to write for my boys; my account says four hundred and four letters for the year I have been here. Every scrap of time is used up to talk to my friends at home on paper, for O, dear! I have so much to say and no confidential earthly friend here, and when I can breathe my thoughts on paper, what a relief!

"Again you ask, 'Do I get all I need?' I am more fortunate than many, as box after box, barrel after barrel comes, and as a general rule, we get along nicely now; but I have an interest in the Barracks that no other nurse has, and many a poor wounded soldier from there comes to me for a sling, a clean shirt, or a pair of socks, or to borrow money, and that is the last I hear from him; and what a comfort it is that I can supply their wants, for they have no female nurse in the Barracks.

"Last week a poor, disconsolate mother who came all the way from Michigan to visit her sick son, came to see me. I found her poor wounded boy was hungry and dirty, and I gave her a comb, jelly, clean clothes, sheets to do up his wounds, lint, and many other things to make them both comfortable; and could you see that mother's look! It seemed as though she never could give kisses enough for my kindness to her.

"There are four hundred in the Barracks, and very bad cases; always when I get an opportunity, I send supplies when we have them to spare. We are surrounded with tents too, and I am amused, sometimes, when a company gets together and they all call me by name, as the woman who sent them what they needed when I had entirely forgotten them. . . . .

"That Jamaica Ginger! could you but see how grateful my wounded boys are for a spoonful of that in hot water when they are in pain. Why, some of them think it is a life preserver. When the surgeon is away I often give them that instead of brandy, and it answers the same purpose."

In the latter part of the month of October, Mrs. Pomroy was allowed a month's furlough, which was a necessity to her, owing to the fatigue induced by the heavy burden of care she had carried for so long a period.

She spent the time with friends in Chelsea,

Newton, and Somerville, and many gatherings were held, both public and private, that friends might have an opportunity to hear of the work she was accomplishing.

She was presented, at this time, with a handsome flag, by the family of Mr. D. of Somerville. A very interesting service was held at the dedication of this flag, in which fervent prayers were offered, that when this cruel war was over, the "soldiers' friend" might return to her home in Chelsea, and bring the flag with her.

It may be well here to give its eventful history from the time it was taken to Columbia College by its happy recipient, and draped around the bay-window of her ward room.

It served as a winding-sheet for hundreds of her brave boys as they were carried from the hospital to their last resting-places. It was not in battle, but had many hair-breadth escapes. Three times it was set on fire; twice by Secessionists.

On the Christmas of 1862 it was decorated by an evergreen border and placed at the entrance hall of the hospital, with pictures of

President Lincoln and General Grant on each side, when a sentinel with a lighted candle carelessly set it on fire; although the evergreen was burned to cinders, the flag was only smoked.

In 1863, at a concert given at Willard's Hall, for the soldiers in the hospitals, the Massachusetts flag was sent to grace the hall. At midnight some rebels broke in, took everything they could lay hands on, and attempted to pull the flag down; but as it was nailed up, they tore holes in it and left it, finding that Massachusetts was not so easily taken. At another time, a traitor found his way into one of Mrs. Pomroy's evening meetings, and lingering about the premises, attempted to set the flag on fire, in the mess-room; but his design was discovered before any damage was done.

At another time, when three hundred of our sick and starving boys were nearly surrounded by the enemy in Virginia, Mrs. Pomroy and other friends visited them, taking food, and clothing, and the flag. When the boys saw the Union signal hoisted in their midst, their surprise and delight knew no bounds. Hunger and hardship for the moment were forgotten, and such cheering as the good old flag of Massachusetts received, with three times three for the owner who dared to raise it on the "sacred soil of Old Virginia!"

Mrs. Pomroy returned to her work invigorated, and writes soon after: "I am once more at home with my boys; not the ones I left, but an entirely new set, some of them Germans; but they all looked bright, and seemed very happy when I entered the room. Most of our wounded men have gone home on furloughs; the convalescents are those who are troubled with rheumatism or heart-disease; many of them young boys from twelve to sixteen."

The Christmas following was kept with royal cheer at Columbia College. Supplies from the North had been very generous. One hundred turkeys were stuffed and roasted, fifty gallons of oysters made into soup, a barrel of cranberry sauce manufactured, and a bountiful supply of pies and vegetables was furnished. Mrs. Lincoln sent flowers, and two barrels of apples. The hospital looked very fine in its holiday aspect.

Mrs. Pomroy's flag, trimmed with evergreen, draped the entrance hall, and all along the wards and halls the boys had ornamented with flowers and evergreens. The Zouaves executed very artistic work in mottoes, stars and wreaths. Never had such an interest been taken before. Surgeons and stewards were on a level with nurses and boys, and the Christmas dinner was pronounced as good as Parker's. The boys marched in by music, some of whom never had seen tables so bountifully spread before.

The mess-room seated four hundred, and was decorated with evergreen and spruce-trees, while mottoes were suspended from tree to tree. After tea, the soldiers' friends from Washington came in, and there was a varied programme of speech-making, anecdotes, and singing from Miss Rumsey. Altogether, they had a "merry Christmas," to make up for some that were not so enjoyable.

The opening year of 1863 was distinguished for the establishment of the President's Emancipation Proclamation, declaring slaves in the United States to be forever free. The Proclamation had received the sanction of Congress, and was issued the previous September, to take effect on the beginning of the New Year. Mrs. Pomroy was stopping at the White House at the time Mr. Lincoln had it under consideration, and had frequent conversations with him about it. He was not unprepared for the terrible denunciations and bitter hatred that were to come from the opposing party, but his stern sense of duty and his hatred of the monstrous evils that grew out of slavery, urged him on to the consummation of that which has been justly called "the greatest event of the nineteenth century."

Nor was opposition apprehended from the South alone. Full well he knew that treason was at his very doors. Washington was full of Secessionists, and the number who prophesied that the Proclamation would only close the doors against the dawning hope of a reaction at the South, were not a few.

One day Mr. Lincoln rode up from the White House to the Soldiers' Home and engaged Mrs. Pomroy in conversation upon the subject. He said:

"I am having a hard struggle; this Proclamation is weighing heavily upon me night and day. I shall encounter bitter opposition, but I think good will come of it, and God helping me, I will carry it through."

The next day, while taking her back to the hospital, it was the sole topic of his conversation. He was more cheerful, for he had finished writing the document the night previous. It was in his hand, and he told her he was going to read it to Charles Sumner, who was his foremost adviser and counselor at this time.

The final Proclamation was celebrated as a great event in many parts of the country, and was the chief topic of conversation around Washington. The organization of the first colored regiment at Beaufort, S. C., was the first outgrowth of this new era.

In Virginia, the Army of the Potomac was nearly at a standstill during the first three winter months, and hospital life at Columbia College wore tediously away in the absence of excitement and the anxieties of previous months.

Mrs. Pomroy was obliged to resort to every means within reach to make the time pass pleasantly. At one time, all the checker-boards and dominoes were in requisition; at another time it was working on cardboard; at another, bead collars were made by the dozen, in which the red, white and blue were tastefully mingled. These were sent North to friends, or to soldiers' fairs, where they were much sought for as soldier relics. Again we see them carving rings from a piece of a rebel's bone, or making chains from laurel wood brought from the woods. Then it was an hour's reading out of some entertaining book, when they would gather round her like children.

She writes to a friend at this time: "I wish you could look in and see my sewing-circle, which meets at three o'clock (genteel hour) in our large room, and notice what a happy time we have in mending the week's socks. I do this for amusement. To see twelve or fourteen men sitting around the bed with scissors and balls of yarn, you would think we were a happy family. They will do most anything, if I will only sit down with them and sew. My sickest boys take great pleasure in Cora's picture books."

These books were none other than Mother Goose melodies, with painted pictures. One little sick fellow, whose mind was nearly gone, clung to the picture of Cock Robin, and would cry inconsolably if it were taken from him.

It was at this time that some ladies from the East sent to Mrs. Pomroy an album quilt which proved one of the great attractions in her ward.

In the white centre piece of each bright-colored square was penned an inscription for the soldier. Some of these were Scriptural, some patriotic, others witty or sentimental. As, "Fear not, Abraham, for I am thy shield and thy exceeding great reward;" and, "Stand! the ground's your own, my braves;" and, "Why are soldiers like tea? Because, when in fire, they are well drawn out," and the like.

A vast store of amusement was stitched into this beautiful piece of work for the lonely patients, and Mrs. Pomroy took great pleasure in showing it to her visitors and sending it through the hospital for all to see; then it was kept for the sickest ones, carried from bed to bed, for an hour at a time, that they might feast their eyes on the bright colors, and read its comforting messages. One poor man who had lost all reason, could only be restrained in his dying hours by having it held up before him to gaze upon.

She writes in the month of January:

"We are still having trouble with our rations, as when we commuted the former steward drew our rations and spent them, cheating us out of two hundred dollars. So now we have to get along the best we can.

"I have just received a letter from my son, saying that he had orders to march across the river, when ammunition, blankets and clothing were taken by the rebel cavalry, and he was left with only the clothing he had on, and almost frozen. . . . . .

"A week ago we were called from our beds at one o'clock, as an invoice of sick men needed our care. They came from Aquia Creek, and were for some time in a regimental hospital. Poor fellows! they could hardly crawl up stairs. One of them said he had not slept on a bed for two years, and he did not believe he could rest on one.

"I am living over my dear husband's sufferings again in the care of a man fifty-nine years old, who has asthma and dropsy. It is hard indeed to look after him with all my other duties. His groans are heard all over the building; he cannot lie down, and he is a sight to behold. His sufferings call up past scenes which I had hoped were almost forgotten. Trained as I have been to suppress all that troubles me, and can stand and see amputations, and close the dying eyes without shedding a tear, yet, when the distress for breath that I was so familiar with for years, falls again on my ears, O, how completely melted down is this frame of mine that I had felt was so strong! . . . . .

"This poor afflicted man was a firm Catholic, and daily counted his beads. On Saturday the priest was sent for to administer the sacrament, as nothing I could say would ease his mind. Father Boyle, a handsome, pompous young priest, dressed in the best of broadcloth, and straw-colored kids, came in and sat down beside him, saying, 'Well, McKinney, what can I do for yea?'

"'Oh,' said the poor sufferer, 'the doctor says I can't live long, and I've got such a load here,' putting his hand on his breast. 'I've been a very wicked man. Can't yer do something for me?'

"'Oh, yes,' said the priest, putting on an elegant purple sash meantime; 'you'll feel better soon.'

"Taking out a prayer-book, he read a Latin prayer.

"'And now don't you feel better?'

"'Oh, no,' said McKinney, groaning in distress of body and soul; 'it's there yet.'

"The priest read another Latin prayer, with no better effect. Then drawing forth a small gold box containing ointment, and a piece of pink cotton, he commenced to anoint his forehead, chin, and the tips of his fingers and toes. 'Now,' he says, 'you are all right. You'll soon be before your judge, and your sins are all forgiven. Now where's your money?'

"The poor fellow instructed me to get it for him, and I gave into his hand fifty dollars. Father Boyle says, 'Now give me that money, and when you die, I'll come and have you well laid out, and give you a good burial in Mount Olivet Cemetery, among the Catholics, and you shall have a handsome stone.'

"McKinney placed the money in his hands, and the priest, making me a very polite salutation, took his leave. Then the poor sufferer directed me to take from his vest pocket a ten dollar bill, and said, 'Here, mother dear, take this and buy something to remember your poor soldier by when he's dead and gone.'

"'McKinney,' I said, 'you know you have a wife and seven children who are very poor, and whom you say you have abused in times past; this money belongs to them, as well as the fifty dollars you gave to Father Boyle. I will write them and send them the money.'

"To this he assented, and I then asked if he felt any better.

"'Oh, no, mistress dear,' he answered, 'the load is still there. Won't you pray for me? I've been such a wicked man, and how can I go before my judge?'

"'But,' said I, 'you thought the priest could forgive you, and would not believe what I read to you, that Jesus Christ alone was the Saviour of sinners.'

"'Oh, read it again, mistress dear, and I will listen,' he said; 'I cannot die with this load here.'

"I read and explained over and over that Jesus was the friend of sinners; that he pitied and forgave the thief on the cross. Finally McKinney dropped the burden that had agonized him so long, by trusting Christ to forgive him, and I called in my Catholic boys to see how easy one could die who trusted alone in the Saviour.

"'It's gone now, mother dear,' he gasped; 'I feel so easy and willing to go.'

"He died; and O, such a relief! His nurse sent for Father Boyle, but he never made his appearance in the hospital after that, and poor McKinney was laid away with no other honors save what was conferred upon him by the Massachusetts flag, beneath whose folds he was carried to his rest. The poor widow received the nurse's letter and money, and sent her a letter full of gratitude and thanks in reply."

Mrs. Pomroy had several lucrative positions offered her while at Columbia College. One, an interest in an orphanage in Philadelphia. The president of the asylum visited her, and Miss Dix urged it upon her as a position that would confer great honor; but she modestly declined, saying that her health was not firm enough to engage in such an undertaking. She was again urged by Miss Dix to accept a position as matron in a fine new hospital at New Haven, Conn. Again, it was to be matron of the Girls' Industrial School, at Lancaster. She says of this last call:

"Doctor Crosby, the surgeon in charge, said he would not let me go. And the boys all exclaimed after their fashion, " Bully for Doctor Crosby!'"

She was urged again to leave the hospital and take charge of the Soldiers' Free Library in Washington, when Mr. Fowle, who had had charge of it, should leave for Boston; but

Doctor Crosby again interposed, and she says, "I have not seen our Brigadier-General Dix about it yet, and I dread to say anything to her."

In spite of the weary round of duties that were fast making inroads upon her physical strength, she put by this proposal of a more easy and congenial service, and kept straight on in the path before her.

In March of 1863, the surgeon, seeing that she needed a change, gave her a few days' furlough, which she spent at the White House. It was at this time Mrs. Pomroy attended the first of a series of receptions, and not willing to share her good fortune alone, she asked and obtained the privilege of inviting her friends from the hospital to have a hand shake with the President, and go throughout the house and conservatory at the next reception.

The invitations were accepted, as may be supposed, with alacrity, and the event was looked forward to with the liveliest anticipations from highest to lowest. The soldiers were instructed by the nurse to provide themselves with clean white gloves, and to look their best.

It was a rare favor for the hard-worked nurses, officers and soldiers of the hospital, and we doubt not their associate was as gratified to obtain the favor as were they to accept it.

During this visit she witnessed at the Capitol the marriage of Mr. John A. Fowle and Miss Elida B. Rumsey, in the House of Representatives, taking with her an exquisite bouquet which Mrs. Lincoln had ordered to be made for the bride. The marriage service was performed by Rev. Mr. Quint, of Jamaica Plain.

"The same evening she attended the dedication of the Soldiers' Free Library, the opening service of which was conducted by the same gentleman. There was speaking by Mr. Fowle and others, and the bride sang, *Flee as a bird to your mountain.*

"On Monday evening," she writes, "was the grandest and largest gathering of the people at the Presidential reception. The whole house was brilliantly lighted and decorated with flowers in the greatest profusion. Long before the hour appointed (eight and one half o'clock) the passages leading into the mansion were crowded

with ladies and gentlemen, and soldiers were stationed at the door to prevent unnecessary crowding. In coming down-stairs and going through the hall to the Blue Room, where the President stood with Mrs. Lincoln, it pleased me to see so many of our brave soldiers, who acted as guards to the doors and halls. There were two officers at each door with muskets; and, I thought, these boys, as well as myself, will never forget this grand reception in war time; and, if there lives are spared, they will tell their children's children of this night. I never saw such a brilliant affair. Crowds of ladies magnificently dressed, leaning on the arms of distinguished men, many of them officers from the military and naval departments, with Generals Fremont and Halleck, Senator Sumner, besides foreign ministers. After shaking hands with the President, the company passed through the Red, Blue and Green rooms, into the large East room, where the promenade commenced, the President and an elegantly dressed lady leading off.

"It was the largest gathering ever known at the White House, and hundreds went away who could not gain admittance. At half-past twelve we were glad to go to our quiet room, for our eyes were satisfied with seeing, and our ears with hearing. After stopping five days at the White House, I came home and found my boys all doing well, pleased not only to see me, but the fine flowers from the conservatory, which reminded them of home and friends."

The following April we may infer that she again detected physical weakness, for she writes: "I must gather up all the strength and energy I can for the next expected battle. Oh, how we are dreading to see the sick and wounded brought to us! Last Sabbath Mr. Lincoln rode up with his family, and invited me to come to the White House and get rested. He says I must not get worn out, for he wants me to live to a good old age."

In her next she writes: "The President sent his carriage for me on Tuesday, and I passed an exceedingly pleasant time until Wednesday, when I became very sick, and had to beg hard to have them take me to my bed in the hospital, for I felt assured that I was going to have a hard sickness, and I did not feel so much at home there as in the College.

"I came home at twelve o'clock, and three physicians were immediately called. After keeping me under the influence of chloroform until twelve, and injecting an opiate in my arm as an experiment, I was at last relieved, although so weak and worn that I came to the conclusion that Woodlawn must open her bosom to receive this poor, feeble clay. After stimulating me so I could speak, I told them that if I did not recover, to have my body embalmed (as they often do the soldiers) and send it to Chelsea; made all necessary arrangements, and through it all felt calm and happy, not knowing what the Lord had in store for me, but leaving all to him to do as he thought best.

"My poor, sick soldiers walked the hall, and for hours waited outside my chamber, saying that they could not go to bed until I was better. Such affection throughout the hospital, the nurses say, has never been seen or felt.

"The President and wife say I must come back to rest when I am able, but you must know I am under military discipline, and we have an High Priestess over us to keep us in charge, so we have to think twice and speak once."

As she gained in health, her letters became more cheerful. She writes: "Hospital life has its pleasures as well as its sorrows, just as life, with all its bitter, has a larger share of sweet, if we only look at it in the right way.

"One of the pleasant things that come to us daily, is the mail, which brings news from home and friends. It is distributed every day, Sunday excepted. When the orderly reads the names on each floor, the soldiers flock around him, and after the letters have been distributed, there is great stillness, for each one is intent on his or her letter.

"While I go my rounds I observe the different countenances. James has a letter from his youngest sister, and one of my sergeants has a letter from *the one* he has told me about, which letter does him more good than medicine, for his has been a long time the *heart disease.* In the corner sits my pet boy, trying his best to make out the words that a poor widowed mother had written, whose early education was limited, and his still more so. Yet he smiles as I ask him, 'From mother?'

"'That it is,' in bold reply; 'and she tells me to prove myself a good soldier, trusting in God, and if I never see her again, she feels that God will take care of her as he has promised.' The big tears roll down his cheeks, as he finally says, 'My poor mother!' and gives me the epistle to read, which seems like gold to him.

"Oh! how often has my heart welled up when my dear boys come to me to read their letters to them; and I, too, can sympathize with those widowed mothers, whose last one has left them to serve his country.

"On the next bed lies my oldest, with hair that indicates the whitening hand of age, and the tear starts as he takes hold of my hand, and tells me his dear wife and children are well; that kind friends have helped them through a hard year of sickness and sorrow, for he had two sons in the army, and one had died. He still keeps on reading the letter, while it seems hard work to tell me, for the tears. 'Yes, she thanks you for writing so often when my life was despaired of, and hopes God's blessing may rest upon you for all you have done for me.' These are the drops of honey that sweeten our pathway, and we enjoy hospital life in war time."

> When peace shall come and hope shall smile again,
> A thousand soldier hearts in Northern climes
> Shall tell their little children, in their rhymes,
> Of the sweet saint who blessed the old war times.

CHAPTER VI.

OUR FATHER KNOWETH.

IN May Mrs. Pomroy's active work among the wounded begins again, as she writes: "We have just taken in and cared for one hundred men, and the worst cases are in my ward. Miss Dix came and wanted me to go with her to Fortress Monroe, as some badly wounded are there, and few of the female nurses can dress wounds; but I have seven men whose lives depend more upon good care than anything else, and the surgeon in charge would not let me off.

"Oh, the work to do, and Saturday night! The business I have to attend to is enough without the wounded."

We cannot doubt this, when we read again that she received calls that week from friends sent by Miss Dix, and Mrs. Wells, from Senators and their wives, sanitary and state agents, beside having the charge of boxes sent to her for distribution.

She writes soon after of visiting the wounded in Cliftburn Hospital, at the request of Miss Dix, who furnished her with money sufficient for their need. She found them in a very filthy condition, and longing to see the face of some woman, as they had only feeble soldiers like themselves to care for them. She obtained some luxuries for the sickest, had them cooked and sent, and says, "How thankful I felt that I could go and do a little, and then interest others in going."

Again she writes: "As my wounded patients are all doing well, Miss Dix invited me to go with her and visit some of the hospitals in Washington. The first one was the Saint Aleosus Hospital, which is under the control of the Sisters of the Sacred Heart.

"This order wear black woollen dresses and capes, white muslin caps or bonnets, with black woollen veils hanging negligently graceful over the back; thick boots and checked aprons. A heavy leaden cross, and quite a large leaden heart, are suspended from the neck. What looking objects to wait upon our sick and dying boys! The surgeons say generally that they prefer Catholics to Protestants, and I feel ashamed to hear that. Many of our Protestant nurses get married, and that troubles Miss Dix and the surgeons.

"I should like to give you a description of the market here. It looks like a dozen old sheds put up, and you can buy all kinds of cottons, as well as fruit, butter, eels, mouse-traps, nails, and the like, all mixed on one stand. The market is closed at two o'clock, and as there are no doors, each one packs up his rubbish, and hand-carts take the articles home till next market day, which is either Saturday or Tuesday."

One of the novelties that grew out of the necessities of the times, was the bakery in the basement of the Capitol. The vault under the Rotunda was used as a storeroom for flour, where eight thousand barrels were sometimes stored. In the vicinity of the fountain were eight ovens, tended by forty bakers, and outside the building were six more double-sized ovens. These ovens were capable, in all, of furnishing sixty-four thousand loaves of bread per day. Day in and day out, these great receptacles turned out their loads of sustenance for the hungry soldiers in the hospital and on the march. And hundreds of sightseers came here to look with wondering curiosity upon this novel exhibit of the exigencies of the war.

The Fourth of July was celebrated at the hospital with unusual demonstration. A fine programme had been arranged by Mr. and Mrs. Fowle, including speeches by prominent men, singing, and martial music. The boys were up and ready by five o'clock in the morning, completing arrangements in the messroom, where the celebration was to be held if the weather proved unfavorable for an out-door meeting. Introductory remarks were made by Mr. Fowle, and Mrs. Fowle sang patriotic airs at frequent intervals.

Among the notable speakers was the brother of John Brown, who was received with immense cheering. The soldiers sang the John Brown song, and *Home, Sweet Home*; a letter from

Governor Andrew was read, expressing heartfelt sympathy and regrets at being unable to be present. Altogether, it was a notable day at "Old Columbia."

Soon after this Mrs. Pomroy was called to the White House to attend upon Mrs. Lincoln, who was suffering from injuries received by a fall from her carriage. It was made evident, afterward, that a plan had been concerted by Secessionists to take the life of the President, on his usual daily drive from the Soldiers' Home to the White House. He had frequently received threatening letters, and the night before this accident, at the instigation of friends, he had consented to take the ride on horseback, with a body-guard of cavalry, consisting of twenty-five men, mounted on picked horses. He accordingly did so, Mrs. Lincoln following shortly after in the carriage. Meanwhile the screws that held the driver's seat in place, had been removed by unknown hands. When at the top of a winding declivity, the seat gave way, precipitating the driver and footman to the ground. The horses became unmanageable, and Mrs. Lincoln, in trying to get from the carriage, was also thrown to the ground, against a sharp stone, receiving a dangerous wound upon the head. She was carried to the nearest hospital, her wounds were dressed, and she was conveyed back to the Soldiers' Home.

Mr. Lincoln, who was sent for from the White House, immediately went for Mrs. Pomroy. She accompanied him at once, and for three weeks was a close attendant, night and day, in the sick room. At the end of that time Mrs. Lincoln so far recovered as to be able to journey, and her nurse, refusing an urgent invitation to accompany her, returned to the hospital, suffering severely in health from her long and close confinement.

During this sojourn in Mr. Lincoln's family, her sympathies were deeply enlisted. Mr. Lincoln went to her in his troubles as to a family friend. An attack upon his person was expected at any time. To Mrs. Pomroy's question, "What will you do about showing yourself in public?" he said, "I can do nothing different from what I am doing; I shall leave it all with my Heavenly Father."

The battle of Vicksburg was raging, and then came the fearful loss of life at Gettysburg, then the battle of Port Hudson. "The Lord have mercy on those poor fellows!" he said, as he walked the floor in an agony of distress. "This is a righteous war, and God will protect the right. Many lives will be sacrificed on both sides, but I have done the best I could, trusting in God. If they gain this important point we are lost, but if we could only gain it, we shall have carried a great point, and I think we shall have a great deal to thank God for; for we have Vicksburg and Gettysburg already."

She said: "Mr. Lincoln, prayer will do what nothing else will; can you not pray?"

"Yes, I will;" while the tears were dropping down his haggard and worn face. "Pray for me;" and he went alone to his room. Could the nation have heard his earnest petition, as the nurse did, they would have fallen on their knees in reverential sympathy.

At twelve o'clock at night, while the soldiers were guarding the house, a sentinel, riding quickly, halted in front of the house, with a telegram, that was carried up to the President. A few moments after, the door opened into the sick room where sat the weary nurse, and the President, standing under the chandelier, with one of his most radiant expressions, said, "Good news! good news! Port Hudson is ours! The victory is ours, and God is good!"

She said, "Nothing like prayer in times of trouble."

He answered, "Yes, O, yes! praise too; for prayer and praise go together."

While an occupant of the White House, a poor widow who had a soldier son lying dead, had tried day after day to see the President, and as often had been repulsed by the ushers on duty. At last she found out Mrs. Pomroy, and poured into her sympathetic ear the story of her troubles.

"Could she see the President, and would he listen to her?"

Mrs. Pomroy promised to see him at once, and he replied to her request:

"Let her come at eight o'clock, immediately after breakfast, and I will hear her the first one."

She came, and told him her sad story, begging that she might have the dead body of her son to take home with her. In tones of sympathy, he said to her:

"God will pity you, and I will give you a note; if it is possible, you may cross the lines, but I am afraid it is not."

Mr. Lincoln felt more than ever his obligation towards Mrs. Pomroy in "saving Mrs. Lincoln's life," (as he told his friends at the White House,) and was ready to grant any request she might deem reasonable.

He took her back to the hospital, as he had done heretofore, with a profusion of flowers heaped in their laps, and in every available space in the carriage, for her soldier boys.

From there she writes: "It does seem to me that God has been trying me, to see where he will put me next. What new experience he will suffer me to pass through is known only to him. Our dear, good President! The Lord bless him, and comfort his poor heart, tried and tempted as he is, and no one to comfort him in times like these. . . .

"I have had a fine young man under my care

for three months, and on Sunday morning he was struck with death. He lingered all day and night, until Monday morning, at half-past one, he died. He leaves a good Christian wife and two little children, besides a large circle of friends to mourn his death. But God did not forget me, even in that trying hour, for my attendant, a little Vermont boy, who is an orphan, came and knelt down at my side, while I was holding the hand of my dying soldier and said, 'Mother, will you pray for me, that God will forgive my sins, and prepare me for death?' Oh, what an hour that was! Every one around us in that large room quietly sleeping, with the full moon looking in upon us, and me, at the dying bed of a fellow soldier, pleading with God for eternal life for the living, while the other was gasping for breath that seemed almost gone. I never felt so near Heaven in my life.

"I miss my dear boy, and his vacant bed speaks to me of suffering; but I am cheered by my little orphan, who now is rejoicing in the Saviour's love."

The boy to whom she refers has been

noticed in a previous letter, having been with her several months. He had been reared among the hills of Vermont, never knowing a mother's love, or remembering a mother's kiss. Ill treated by his grandparents, with no knowledge of reading or writing, he ran away and enlisted, and was brought into the hospital in a sick and wounded condition. Mrs. Pomroy was kind to him, and when he became her attendant, she taught him to read and write, so that in the month of July he could pen her a letter after his own weak fashion, to speak the love and gratitude with which he requited her.

We trust this letter will not seem too trivial for perusal, voicing, as it did, the loyal devotion of many a poor soldier's heart, unable to express it, even in this poor, faltering way.

COLUMBIA COLLEGE HOSPITAL,
WASHINGTON, D. C., July 14, 1863.

DEAR MOTHER:—And indeed can I call thee dear mother? With your pre-consent it is indeed a great pleasure to call you so, if it would not be obnoxious to you. I have loved and respected that title since I was old enough to know the need of a mother's love and soothing words, to cheer him in his sadness and melancholy moods. Neither have I known the worth of a mother until you used me with so much kindness;

you could not used me better under any considerations; but, mother, I have not done by you as I have been done by; but I hope hereafter that if I am permitted to stay here with you, that I shall conduct myself as a faithful and dutiful son should to his affectionate mother. "May the Lord Jesus" be with me, and give me a good heart: such a one that shall be good in his sight, and in Mrs. R. R. Pomroy's sight, and that she can love.

Affectionate mother! And, indeed, will she be my own dear mother? Little does she think how that word sounds in my ears.

O Father! do bless Mrs. Pomroy, and may she have a good heart, one that will beat to thee, and to thy cause, and may she love the motherless DeWitt next to her own son. And, Father in Heaven, wilt thou be with me, and give me a good heart, so that I may find favor both in thy sight, and in Mrs. R. R. Pomroy's, too. And may I be faithful and dutiful as a humble Christian in thy sight, whether I am in the world's sight or not. And may we love each other as both mother and son, and may it be a holy affection in thy sight. God be with thee, and give you strength to bear your trials and afflictions with meekness, and patience, and a Christian fortitude. God be with thee, and bless thee, dear Mother Pomroy. I ask for the Lord Jesus Christ's sake, in his name. Amen. DEWITT RAY.

N. B. And if I have offended you by calling you mother, by letting me know it, I will not ever commit the same offence again. Yours, and may the Lord bless thee, dear mother. D. W. R.

Mrs. Pomroy soon lost her faithful attendant, as she writes later: "I have now an invalid for an attendant, and I hope to reclaim him, as he looks like — well, no matter. With God all things are possible.

"My dear little orphan said to me, as I took his hand for the last time, 'Mother, if I die on the battle-field now, I have found two good friends, a Christian mother and a loving Saviour.' How my heart melted at those words. I feel lonely without him."

She never saw her loyal-hearted boy again. He died at his post; shot instantly through the head while guarding a rifle-pit in the far-away South. His open Bible, found upon his bed, just as he had left it to go on duty, indicated that in his last hours he was faithful to his God as to his country. In his vest pocket next his heart, was found a picture of Mrs. Pomroy, inscribed on the back: "My own dear mother, Mrs. R. R. Pomroy, Chelsea, Mass."

His captain took the picture, inclosed it in a letter to her, in which he speaks of his excellent character and example, and describes his death. Mrs. Pomroy received it while on her next furlough, in the month of October, and set out at once to his mountain home in

Vermont, to carry the information to his grandparents, and to take to them the money and keepsakes he had left in her possession.

Arrived at the lonely little town, she found her way, by inquiry, to a little red house on the top of the hill, where DeWitt's home had been. She was invited in, and asked to take a seat on the settle by the large, old-fashioned fireplace. Then she commenced inquiries about their grandson. They spoke of him with evident pride.

"He has been in a hospital," they said, "and he has learned to read and write, and writes us beautiful letters about a dear mother he has found there who has taught him everything; and, strangest of all, he has got religion."

And they took the worn package of letters from their accustomed place to verify the truth of their assertion.

Mrs. Pomroy then made herself known; told them she was the "mother" of whom he had written, and then the sad news of his death. The poor old couple could scarcely believe her. Tears of sorrow and gratitude were mingled in one as they clasped her hand in wonderment at the story of his life and death.

"John," said the old lady, "harness up the horse and go round and get the neighbors." Preparations were made for a gathering, and towards night the room was completely filled, although the nearest neighbor lived a half-mile distant.

They looked with wondering curiosity upon a woman who had passed two years in a Southern hospital; who had seen and taken care of DeWitt, and had taught him how to write those fine letters which he had sent home. But when she told them the sad scenes of her hospital life, how DeWitt had sought and found the Saviour, and the change that had come over the wild, wayward boy they used to know, when he was brought under the influence of the Divine Spirit, it was too much for their fortitude. Many a tear was wiped away by the worn coat-sleeve; many a woman's face was buried in her handkerchief before the recital closed. Then there was a season of prayer, such as had not been known by them for a long time.

They begged her on going away to stay among them for a week. But she felt obliged to go the next morning, and leave the seed she had dropped into the hearts of these humble people to take root, not knowing what the harvest should be, until the end of all things.

Next day the horse was again harnessed, and the old man took her to the nearest country store, where he purchased for her a simple gold ring, as a reminder of the motherless DeWitt whom she had befriended.

Mrs. Pomroy spent her second furlough in the companionship of friends, as before, attending several public gatherings. Among the most noticeable of these was one held in Salem, at the residence of Senator H——.

She had met him in the hospital through the agency of the President, who told Mr. H—— that there was a good Massachusetts woman in Columbia College, who was the best friend he had found, and urged him to go and see her. Mr. H—— went, accordingly, and made her acquaintance, inviting her to come to Salem on her next furlough and visit his family.

She accepted the invitation, and received here every attention.

Having left the dinner-table, she was surprised at the frequent ringing of the door-bell. The occasion of it was evident later, when a room full of ladies and gentlemen were presented to her, and she was invited to speak to them upon her hospital work, and her experience at the White House. Question followed question until her voice grew faint through exhaustion and she was left to the quiet of her own room.

At this time occurred the loss of her journal. While passing through the crowded streets of Boston in a friend's carriage, they stopped to witness the passing of a company of soldiers. The journal was stowed away, together with money, a gold watch-chain, and other valuables, in a bag at the bottom of the carriage. No suspicion of the loss was entertained until she reached home, when it was found to be missing, and no amount of inquiry or advertising ever served to restore it.

She felt this misfortune like the loss of a friend, for in its pages were recorded passages the most interesting of her life's history; events that she had confided solely to its keeping, which no effort of memory could ever recall, so closely did one event crowd upon another in the span of those two eventful years. She makes frequent allusion to it in letters that followed her return. At one time:

"I mourn my journal, as there is not a day passes but I have occasion to look in it. This is really a sad affliction, but I try to feel some good may come of it after a while."

And again: "Perhaps I was planning too much for the future about my journal, for I did mean to give some parts of it to the public. But the Lord will take care of me, without my being anxious for the morrow."

Her first letter on her return was written for the *Chelsea Telegraph and Pioneer*, which we give as follows:

WASHINGTON, October 28, 1863.

MR. MASON:—I arrived safely at my place of duty last evening, and as I entered the lower hall I was greeted with, "Welcome Home!" As I farther advanced, up on the fourth floor I heard well-known voices exclaim, "Mother has come!" and I never saw happier faces as I shook hands with each of them, and listened to their tales of suffering, and their counting the days when I should be at home. I do not know which was the most happy, the boys or myself, for they clustered around me like my own family to know if I had come back to stay, and like questions. I found all doing well but two, who had been confined to their beds for some time; and a third, who has a ball in his back, on whom an operation was performed yesterday, but without finding the ball. He has been a sufferer for five months, and is one of my three *white* boys who are learning to read. I make the distinction of color, because I am teaching three contrabands their letters — a class of six, all of them over twenty, just learning to read.

There has been but little change since I left, excepting the removal of Mr. and Mrs. Fowle to Boston, which we all regret very much, as they have been unwearied in doing for our brave boys what no one else would have done. The sweet songs that Mrs. Fowle sung often kindled our patriotism when the fire was getting rather low, for we have to talk about the war and sing patriotic songs to *some*, or they would have none at all on getting up from a sick bed.

The first sound that greeted my ear this morning was the muffled drum and fife, telling us that another of our brave boys was to be laid away in the "Soldiers' Home," where are laid already over eight thousand of those we hold so dear. I have often visited the spot, and could never help shedding tears for the dear ones at home, some of whom, perhaps, may never know where father, husband, or brother are laid, for in passing along I have often observed on the walnut slabs that mark these graves, this inscription, *Unknown*.

During the last two years in this place, I have had under my charge five hundred and seven boys, and have lost by death only thirty-one, and only two of those from wounds. I feel to bless God that he has given me health and a willing mind to do his work.

The nurse is comforted by the sweet thought that friends are sustaining her in her many trials by oft-repeated tokens and many prayers, and who have shown so much sympathy toward her in view of the recent loss of her journal. She takes courage from the lesson of the spider, whose house is often pulled down, still to persevere in a *new journal*, and with God's grace assisting her to commence on a new year with greater zeal and endure like a good soldier the trials that may come, feeling that sunshine will succeed the clouds, as it has thus far along life's journey, and that God would use her in his own way to comfort the sick and dying, who shall sacrifice their lives for their country.

R. R. P.

In November she writes: "We have had more new nurses, and such doings! Then so many new ward-masters ordering us round. The work is getting hard, and were it not for the sake of my boys, I should be tempted to leave. I wish you could know how our poor fellows are treated, and if I were not here to take their part, they would fare much worse. . . . . Mrs. Secretary Wells sent some pickled beets to me yesterday, and what a luxury it was to the poor sick ones! I fed them once round with it, a slice at a time, then round the second time, then went to the lower floor and did the same.

"I have had a visit from the novel-writer, Mrs. Southworth, and have also spent an afternoon with her, in her pretty house at

Georgetown. Her son is a surgeon on my ward. .... The surgeon in charge told me yesterday that all the worst cases brought into the hospital were to be put in my ward, as he had full confidence in me as a careful nurse; and more than that, he has left his pocket case of instruments, for me to probe or get out small pieces of bone, also to plug the wounds when necessary."

In a letter dated November 23, she writes: "At two last night two hundred wounded came to the hospital and seventy-five more were brought in on stretchers. Our beds are filled, and some have to sleep on the floor."

It was not uncommon at night time to see beside the beds here and there, the wooden legs or arms of the sleeping occupants. But this, like all other hospital spectacles, became so common that it ceased to shock the most fastidious. One poor fellow, who had left his leg on the battle-ground of Fair Oaks, whittled out his own wooden leg while in the hospital, and became so happy and resigned in the possession of it that he recorded his satisfaction in verse, as follows:

L-E-G (ELEGY) ON MY LEG.

Good leg, thou wast a faithful friend,
    And truly hast thy duty done;
I thank thee most that to the end
    Thou didst not let this body run.

Strange paradox! that in the fight
    Where I of thee was thus bereft,
I lost my left leg for "the right,"
    And yet the right's the one that's left.

But while the sturdy stump remains,
    I may be able yet to patch it;
For even now I've taken pains
    To make an L-E-G to match it.

In November, Mrs. Pomroy writes again to Mr. Mason as follows: "When I arrived home I had to report myself to the surgeon in charge, and also to Miss Dix, who seemed pleased to see me back again, and asked me if I knew of any ladies from Massachusetts, who would like to come as nurses.

"I told her there were several whom I knew would like to come, but they could not with her ideas of nurses. Why! she thought they were plain and easy. They surely are, and I will give a few of them for those who are contemplating the subject.

"They must know how to cook all kinds of low diet (for in Columbia the nurses have always done that). She would like to have them wear brown, black, or drab dresses, very small hoops, no curls, no jewelry, nor flowers on their bonnets. They must look neat themselves, and keep their boys and wards the same. Must write and read for their boys, but not for any book or *newspaper;* must strictly obey all the rules and regulations of the hospital; must be in their own room at taps, or nine o'clock, unless obliged to be with the sick; must not go to any place of amusement in the evening; must not walk out with any private or officer; must not allow a private or officer in their own room except on business; must be willing to take the forty cents per day that is allowed by government, to assist them in supplying what the rations (or eighteen cents per day) will not furnish in food; pay for their own washing, shoes and clothing; and then, if there is a *surplus*, it is expected that it will be spent upon the soldiers, to make them comfortable, for no nurse must come into the service with the idea of laying up one cent.

"She wants all who are under her supervision to be self-denying, self-sacrificing, with a large heart and open hand, to follow her example in doing all they can for the soldier.

"She is worthy of imitation, as she is seen on the battle-fields binding up wounds or giving stimulants, or stopping hemorrhage till a surgeon can come, or giving them food in cases of almost starvation.

"She also wants good Christian women, who can be mothers to our dying boys, for often the question is asked, 'Will you pray for me?' Hard it must be for the dying to have no one to offer consolation or breathe a prayer for him who will soon be beyond the sound of mortal voice.

"Also all who may apply must be educated, intelligent, and with a large share of patience, forbearance and sobriety; quiet, careful not to offend, being willing rather to suffer wrong than to do wrong, adding Paul's exhortation, 'As far as in you lieth, live peaceably with all men.'"

The editor adds the following postscript: "Is it not unjust to require these noble-hearted women to make such unwonted sacrifice, without reasonable pay, while every he that wears a shoulder-strap or performs any sort of service whatever, has his appropriate reward?"

It may be well to add in this connection that Miss Dix's promise of a squat of land to all those nurses who had done faithful service in the war, was never realized; and the instances are comparatively few where any emolument has ever accrued to them in remuneration for their untiring services.

In a letter that follows, in the month of November, she gives a history of the routine of hospital life as follows: "There has been an invoice of wounded brought to us since I last wrote you, and seventy were brought in on stretchers. They are from Stonington Junction.

"Since they have come to the hospital, they seem cheerful and happy. Some say they have seen hard service and hard fare, without one kind word since they left home, which has been two years.

"Would like to have you look into my large room on Saturday morning and spend the day and see the routine of work. The reveille is played at five, and all who are able to get up, must make their beds, wash, and be ready at the drum-call, at six o'clock, for breakfast. The nurses have theirs at seven. Making of beds, sweeping and dusting done, the attendant brings up the breakfast for those who are not able to get up. After this, two boys wash the dishes, two sweep the rooms, two wash the spittoons, while two contrabands empty the slops. Then commences the dressing of wounds, making the boys comfortable, some sitting in bed reading, others playing checkers, while quite a number are getting ready to go to their regiments. Several are being shaved, others having their hair cut, while another is watering my flowers.

"At eight, the surgeon's call with drum and fife, when everything must be in order. Then come the orders for medicines, soap, crackers, etc., for not a thing is allowed without an order from the surgeon of the ward.

"After wounds are dressed, blisters, plasters

and medicines attended to, the Bible is read; and here a boy takes his from his pocket, and tells how it saved his life when shot through the lungs, and it parried the force of the blow.

"At eleven o'clock the medicines come up from the dispensary, and while administering them, a number of invalids came up four flights of stairs to see a bead bag from Chelsea, made by a widow lady, whose only son fell a sacrifice in this cruel war.

"At twelve o'clock the drum beats, and all go to the mess-room for dinner. Company almost always at noon, and unless we go at the time, we either lose our dinner, or it is cold. But there is a carriage, and the lady calls for the nurse on the upper floor. She knows the ward well, for her feet were the first to bring the little luxuries that my sickest boys had.

"It is Mrs. Secretary Wells, with her large tin pails; one with pickles and onions, and the other with baked apples. We can afford to go without our dinner, as our boys will enjoy so much; it is such a comfort to go through the hospital, and give to the desponding and sickest, those delicacies. How kindly she speaks to the boys, cheering them by her smile, and giving them books and papers.

"After the dinner is through, our sewing circle meets; then all my boys get round a bed, and the socks are mended. It is amusing to see the pain as well as pleasure they manifest, as each tugs to outdo the other. There are sometimes twenty-five pairs to mend, and that helps the nurse.

"At five o'clock the drum calls for supper. After that the wounds are dressed, then at seven the surgeons call, when sleeping powders, poultices, etc., are administered. At half-past eight the drum beats for all to be in bed, at nine the bells ring (or taps), then lights are extinguished, and all conversation ceases, while the nurse arranges the medicine for the watchers. So ends the week."

Mrs. Pomroy, in company with friends, spends a day in Virginia this month, visiting, among other places of interest, Arlington House, General Lee's residence. The road thither presented a desolate aspect; no houses to be seen for miles; acres of trees felled, and nothing of interest, save the forts that had been erected by our Union soldiers to protect Washington.

The house and grounds of General Lee were guarded by Union men. Orders were posted in all quarters, forbidding any damage to be done, even to the picking of a flower.

Mrs. Pomroy wanted a memento, and knowing one of the sentinels to be a Massachusetts man, she said to him, "I am a Massachusetts woman; won't you let me have one from among all these?" pointing to a large bed of flowers close by.

The sentinel eyed her with a knowing look, and then said: "I am forbidden to give away anything here, but I'll turn my back, and you may do what you please."

He did so, and she bore away a souvenir of that once proud but fallen estate.

Going inside they found some of the house servants still in the old quarters. Aunt Sallie, the mother of only nineteen children, too feeble and decrepit to leave the old home, was interviewed. All of her children, save one, had been taken from her and sold into slavery.

The iron had entered deep into her soul, as every lineament of her worn and wrinkled visage bore evidence.

"Massa Lee powerful hard at de whippin' post," she said.

Sad stories were told of wrongs and cruelty committed here.

At another time she witnessed a touching spectacle, when the Invalid Corps, nine thousand in number, went to the White House, to present themselves to the President for his inspection. All the way from Meridian Hill to the White House, a distance of two miles, thronged this legion of heroes from the battlefield, minus an arm, minus both arms, minus hands and feet, minus a leg, crippled, halt, walking on crutches, with slings and empty coat sleeves, but bearing proudly these marks of honor, such as no distinction of money or rank could confer upon them.

Again, she chronicles another sad day, when the Gettysburg burial-ground was dedicated. All flags from every fort, hospital and public building were at half-mast, while the mock funeral, with the booming of cannon, the slow and solemn tread of the soldiers, with arms reversed, keeping time to the funeral dirges, vividly conscious that themselves and numbers of others out of this vast concourse of followers must share the same fate before the close of another year, added to the solemnity of a scene never to be forgotten.

>If, for the age to come, this hour
>Of trial hath vicarious power,
>And, blest by thee our present pain
>Be Liberty's eternal gain,
>Thy will be done.

CHAPTER VII.

I AM WITH YOU ALWAY.

HER journal records the following for Wednesday, November 25: "Busy this morning, and in the afternoon received two boxes from Salem, with all the fixings for a Thanksgiving dinner, expressly for the nurses, from the ladies of the Tabernacle Church. Two roast turkeys, plum pudding, pies, all kinds of cake, cookies and crackers, fruit, jellies, wines, etc. All was nicely cooked, and we received it with overflowing hearts. Our gifted Mrs. R. has been chosen from among the nurses, to respond in fitting terms. The matron, with Mrs R. and myself, kept this dinner for a surprise to the other nurses.

"I went into Mrs. R.'s ward that day, to see a dying soldier who wished to speak to me. He took my hand and looked upward as though he were praying God to bless me. He then asked me to sing *Happy Day*, and *Am I a Soldier of the Cross?* trying to beat time with his emaciated hand. Then I tried to sing *Softly now the Light of Day*. When I had done, I thought he was gone, but he put his hands together and said, 'Jesus, I am coming home,' and then died."

December 1st she writes: "I feel that I am working rather too hard, as my attendant is very sick; but whenever the thought comes over me, 'How can I leave till this cruel war is over?' the answer comes, 'Let Him do as seemeth best.' I have lately been thinking that the day is not far distant when I shall lay my burden down."

A little later on, she writes to a friend: "Truly another Thanksgiving has passed, and with it trials and many sorrows. I am sitting sad and lonely in my little room, wishing I could gather some of my dear friends at home around me, and relieve my mind of its load. Yes, we as a band of self-sacrificing women are made a reproach to others. I cannot write all the particulars, but I will give you a few hints.

"In the first place, we nurses had a good Thanksgiving dinner; and if ever praise and thanksgiving went up from human hearts, it truly did in the old mess-room, by the nurses, for God's unspeakable goodness in leading others more highly favored, to think of us. We felt to go on with our duties more zealously, for as the body is strengthened, so are we the better able to do our whole duty; for you know not half the disagreeable things that fall to our lot among these sick boys. Well, there has been quite a breeze about the nurses having turkey, etc. The steward has said that the boxes came for the boys' dinner only, and the nurses had no right to use them. Accordingly, I had the letter from Salem read, and that did not satisfy, and as I was the receiver, I am yoked with all the others in using things sent to the boys.

"Then again, a lady who is not friendly to Miss Dix called to see me, and, although a perfect stranger, asked me what I thought Miss Dix would say, if she knew I wrote for a paper. She thought if Miss Dix ever saw those papers she would make a stir.

"I can truly say I was dumb. I opened not my mouth, for she was a Massachusetts woman, and a lion in manner.

"During all this my attendant has been very sick, and my surgeon, taking pity upon my care-worn looks, wrote for help immediately. I was sent a poor invalid, lame, with sore eyes, and who had the use of but one hand. The surgeon came to my room, saw my distress, said I was too sick to be round, and told me to stay in my room for a week, and he would make things right. The sick boy was sent to his company, and not an attendant have I had in his place yet, although two weeks have passed.

"Then, three of the nurses have had trouble with the ward master, and three others with the commissary, and now the surgeon in charge has come down on us all, and Old Columbia is getting to be rather warm for the nurses, and several are thinking about leaving.

"A note was sent to my surgeon, saying: 'Nothing but a clerk or a gentleman would answer Mrs. Pomroy; for she tried to have them all gentlemen under her, and treated them as though they were, when she ought to remember that they were nothing but privates, and ought to be treated as such.'

"Well, I always do forget their rank in the army, as long as I know they are brave boys.

"This is the beginning of trouble on my third year, and unless my back and side get stronger, there will have to be a change. Tread on a worm and it will turn; and poor, frail human nature cannot stand everything. Do not think I have lost my interest in the poor soldier; oh, never for a moment! Could you see what I have to, your whole soul would go out for them."

But there was another ordeal in store for her. She had, at this time, some boys reduced very low by sickness, who needed something besides the coarse food provided for them. One wanted some chicken broth, and another some tomatoes. She sent down to the steward to know if they could be had. He gave her attendant a curt refusal, saying that she made altogether too much of her boys, and that she was an extravagant nurse.

General ———'s wife visited her that day, and asked on leaving what she could do for her. On being told the needs of these sick boys, she said, "Wait a few hours and I will send you the tomatoes and broth ready for use."

Time passed, and the lady in her elegant carriage drove up. The footman, with his pail of broth in one hand, and his basket of tomatoes in the other, with a beautiful bouquet of flowers, was about entering the hospital, when he was met by the surgeon in charge, who accosted him gruffly, saying, "What are you going to do with these things?"

"Take them up to Mrs. Pomroy's room, for her sick boys," he replied.

The surgeon then forbade it, saying there was euough in the hospital to feed the boys on, and ordered the things put back in the carriage.

The lady went home justly indignant at this insult. Her husband and friends were informed of her treatment, and as a result, an article appeared next day in the *Washington Morning Chronicle* regarding disturbances that had taken place at Columbia College.

Mrs. Pomroy heard the newsboys crying the

sensation of the day underneath her window, sent down and purchased a paper and read an account of the affair well set out, with indignant comments upon the state of things at Columbia College.

The news was not long in reaching Miss Dix. She at once visited Mrs. Pomroy, and aksed for an explanation. The truth stated, Miss Dix said, "There will be an investigation, and you will have to give evidence before military officers, together with the other nurses; but don't flinch; you are in the right, and you will come out victorious. If you have to leave, I can find other places for you." To the other nurses she gave injunctions to "Tell the truth, and nothing but the truth."

The morning of the examination arrived. Mrs. Pomroy's trunk was packed ready to be sent to the White House, where she expected to go. The nurses were called down one by one, and she last of all. A large attendance of officers, including a medical inspector and medical director, were present, and received her with marked politeness. She was then closely questioned as to her family and age, why she left home to go into a hospital, and much more. She answered in her usual quiet and dignified manner, feeling, as she said, "Not afraid to face any of them," so strong was she in the truth and righteousness of her cause.

They inquired, "Have you been obliged to send home for anything?"

"Oh, yes; many times."

"And for what?"

"Sugar, rice, tea, coffee, wine, etc."

"How much have you had sent?"

"A great many barrels and boxes full. My friends have been glad to supply me, and I have always shared with the other nurses, and sent them outside the hospital, where they were needed."

"Have you ever sent for crackers?"

"Yes, often. Frequently my boys would have only two crackers apiece, and some weak tea, and I felt they needed more to make them strong again. When I had a barrel come I sent them round to all the soldiers."

After finishing their investigation, the officers dismissed her with every mark of respect.

As a result both the surgeon in charge and steward were removed from the hospital, while Mrs. Pomroy received the congratulations of friends who were overjoyed at the sudden turn of events.

The remainder of the year 1863 was passed more quietly, with now and then an influx of wounded men and an occasional visit to the White House, or a trip into the surrounding country to get supplies for the table or the sick boys, that could not be obtained otherwise. Christmas passed with festivities suited to the day; the boys all had a good Christmas dinner, and there was a flag-raising, with speeches and music.

She speaks in her journal of going to Alexandria, and visiting the church where Washington used to worship, and of seeing the battery and the great gun which faced the Potomac, that weighed two thousand five hundred pounds; of visiting a convalescent camp, and the Freedman's village, where some hundreds of contrabands lived and worked on General Lee's farm. They seemed very happy, " bressing Massa Lincoln for freedom."

She had frequent intercourse with the contrabands in the hospital. They were employed to do the most menial services, and her sympathies were strongly enlisted in their behalf. We find her busy in her spare moments, teaching them to read from primers that had been sent her from the North. They never wearied of telling her about their slave life and of calling down blessings upon the head of their beloved President.

"Hope Massa Lincoln hab' the highest seat in Hebben," was their fervent exclamation.

The cold, short days now coming on were very depressing to the poor invalids who had lain for weeks, with little to look forward to. Mrs. Pomroy now planned an entertainment for them through these contraband followers.

While visiting at the White House, old aunt Mary said to her, "I wants ye to see my son Sammy; he's powerful smart on de bones."

"What is that?" said Mrs. Pomroy.

"Why, he plays in der colored band, and dey say it's der finest in Washington."

Mrs. Pomroy expressed her desire to meet

Sammy and hear the band, and aunt Mary arranged a meeting for the next evening. She was introduced to Sammy, and invited him to come with the members of his band to entertain her boys. At the appointed time they made their appearance with a full equipment of banjos, bones and triangles, and gave such a programme as made sick and well catch an inspiration of mirth, that was better than medicine, better than a sermon, better than anything else within reach; and the surgeon exclaimed:

"What will Mrs. Pomroy do next for her boys?"

When the New Year came round, they had settled down to making bead collars again and mending socks. The following lines were found in one of the socks, sent by a "Lively Old Lady" in New Hampshire; and while they mended, Mrs. Pomroy was often called on to read it.

> By the fireside cosily seated,
>   With spectacles riding her nose,
> The Lively Old Lady is knitting
>   A wonderful pair of hose.

She pities the shivering soldier,
  Who is out in the pelting storm,
And busily plies her needles
  To keep him hearty and warm.

Her eyes are reading the embers,
  But her heart is off to the war,
For she knows what those brave fellows
  Are gallantly fighting for.
Her fingers as well as her fancy
  Are cheering them on their way,
Who, under the good old banner,
  Are saving their country to-day.

She ponders how, in her childhood,
  Her grandmother used to tell
The story of barefoot soldiers,
  Who fought so long and well.
And the men of the Revolution
  Are nearer to her than us,
And that, perhaps, is the reason
  Why she is toiling thus.

She cannot shoulder a musket,
  Nor ride with cavalry crew,
But nevertheless she is ready
  To work for the boys who do.
And yet in "Official Despatches,"
  That come from the army or fleet,
Her *feats* may have never a notice,
  Though ever so mighty the *feet*.

So prithee, proud owner of muscle,
  Or purse-proud owner of stocks,
Don't sneer at the labors of woman,
  Or smile at her bundle of socks.
Her heart may be larger and braver
  Than his who is tallest of all,
The work of her hands as important
  As cash that buys powder and ball.

And thus while her quiet performance
  Is being recorded in rhyme,
The tools in her tremulous fingers
  Are running a race with time.
Strange that four needles can form
  A perfect triangular bound;
And equally strange that their antics
  Result in perfecting "The round."

And now, while beginning "To narrow,"
  She thinks of the Maryland mud,
And wonders if ever the stocking
  Will wade to the ankle in blood.
And now she is "Shaping the heel,"
  And now she is ready "To bind,"
And hopes if the soldier is wounded,
  It never will be from behind.

And now she is "Raising the instep,"
  Now narrowing off at the toe,
And prays that this end of the worsted
  May ever be turned to the foe.

> She gathers the last of the stitches,
> As if a new laurel were won,
> Now placing the ball in the basket,
> Announces the stocking is done.

We extract from a letter, written January 18th, the following reference to trouble growing out of a want of harmony among the nurses.

"Many trying duties of late have worn upon me, especially trouble about the hospital clothing, that really needed mending; and do not think it egotism in me when I tell you I took the responsibility, and advised that all the nurses take some garments every week, till our four hundred shirts and over three hundred pairs of socks, were mended, for I felt that we as nurses ought to look after those articles — many of them sent from Northern homes, and cotton so high, to say nothing of labor and time. It seemed to me that a heavy responsibility was resting on this favored hospital, and, God giving me words .of wisdom, I would speak.

"There are always some who never mend for themselves at home, and they say they did not come to a hospital to mend old clothes, but only to look after the sick. How great the patriotism of some, when they come to do the poor soldier good, and cannot condescend to mend a shirt to put on his back when sick or wounded, or mend a pair of socks to cover those poor feet that have travelled miles on the battle-field — yes, and even tracked it with *blood*, to save this, our country, from ruin. 'Consistency, thou art a jewel!'"

A few months previous to this, the hospital was blessed with the presence of a dear little girl. It happened in this way.

A poor sick man who belonged to the invalid corps on Meridian Hill, was in the early stages of consumption and used frequently to speak to Mrs. Pomroy of his wife and child, living in New York. He longed to see them, but all visits from far away friends were denied. One day he ventured to say to her, "I wish my wife could come here in some service; then I could see her once in a while. She is strong and well, and used to work."

Mrs. Pomroy bethought her of a change needed in the nurses' cook-room, at the hospital, told him to keep up courage and she would see what could be done. She consulted the matron and nurses, who were willing to try the New York woman as an experiment, and she was sent for and came, bringing little Caty, three years old.

Now a child was an unheard-of thing in Columbia College, and at first she was kept in a very quiet way, down in the cook's room, for fear the surgeon should see her and order away both mother and child.

Little Caty was a sweet creature, and soon won the affection of all the nurses, and, child-like, would flit out of doors to get a stolen look at her father on the hill, and exchange greetings with the poor, infirm soldiers who were out walking in the sunshine, trying to gain strength.

One morning she put her little hand in Mrs. Pomroy's, and asked if she might go up and see the soldiers. Mrs. Pomroy said, "You may go up in my room and stay a little while, but I can't let you go any further." But after a time, by childlike persistency, she found her way into the large ward-room, and here she was adopted at once into the home and hearts of the soldier-boys, who, many of them, had just such little ones at home.

She was like a beam of sunshine; her sweet face and childish prattle, her touching sympathy for all the wounded and sick, brightened many weary, homesick hearts, and when she was absent for a day, the men would ask, "When are you going to bring Caty up again?"

Arrangements had been made on New Year's to make her several presents. Busy fingers at the North were fashioning a little crimson dress and some aprons for the occasion. But one day the little pet was missing. The boys were told that she was ailing; a week passed, and there came word that she was very sick with diphtheria. She died that night in Mrs. Pomroy's arms.

Every face was sad the next morning throughout the hospital. They laid her away that day, in a tiny casket which the nurses had bought, robed her in the crimson dress, with flowers from the White House. The steward willingly vacated his room that she might rest there, while the inmates of the hospital came in to look upon her for the last time. It was a touching sight to see the sick and disabled, one by one, young and old, all who could hobble in on canes and crutches, come and shed tears over the lovely waxen figure and kiss her as though she belonged to them. Even the surgeons, who had learned to look on suffering unmoved, shed tears over the coffin, as they recognized in her one of God's angels too good for earth.

The sick father obtained a week's furlough, and Mrs. Pomroy accompanied the sorrowing parents with the body of little Caty on their way home as far as the Baltimore depot. The father came back, but to die. A few months, and he, too, was carried home and a new grave was made beside the little one.

Mrs. Pomroy writes during the winter months: "This has been a trying season to us all, for we have nothing but convalescents, and they are far more trouble than when confined to the bed by sickness or wounds. They are very uneasy, going to the sutlers and buying those things that bring on sickness. Many of them get passes to go to Washington, which is the worst place I know for young men: there they get intoxicated, and, if they overrun their pass, they are put in the guardhouse till next morning.

"Since General Grant has taken command, the men seem to feel encouraged. He has ordered many of the officers who were to be seen round the public houses, to their regiments, and is calling in all the ambulances that can be seen through the streets of Washington, for government use. After this, we shall not see quite so many officers with their friends, riding through our city, when they should be in the field; for, visit the capital when you would, it seemed thronged with those who were able to be where General Grant has now put them.

"So far we say, 'Good for Grant!' We hope he is the 'Coming man' come; but God only knows. The 'Battle Cry' is sounding in our ears; it is the first sound that greets us in the morning, and the last at night, for as we look out from our windows and see workmen putting up a large number of tents, we ask, What can all this mean?

The answer is, An order has come to Columbia College Hospital to enlarge her borders, and make ready to accommodate *one thousand wounded patients:* and as we look over to Carver Hospital, the work of putting up more tents is going on, so as to accommodate *fourteen hundred more* wounded men; and then on our right, they are making the same preparation. Can we help at times feeling sad, as we see all this going on? Can we help feeling strong sympathy for the loved ones at home, who have friends in this dreadful war?

"Friends at the North, pray for us; for when the next battle comes it will be a hard one; and we have our work to do. God grant that we may have strength equal to our day; that we may never flinch from duty, but prove ourselves *true women* — true to ourselves, our country, and our God.

"We have had several deaths within a few weeks from typhoid, and a few from small-pox. Two of the typhoid patients had their mothers come to see them; and although this was forbidden, we could not turn them away from the bedsides of their sick sons. One of them was from my own native State, and a few hours before he died, as he was delirious, the mother in the greatest agony said, 'If my poor Charlie could only know that I was here, and would say something that I could tell my family, it would be such a comfort.'

"The surgeons had done all in their power, and we all felt that vain was the help of man. But in the evening Charlie became conscious, and told his mother he had prepared, while on the field, to meet death, and all was well with him. He was taken home, where father, mother, sisters and brother could see his lifeless form.

"And the other mother — this was indeed sad, for he was her only son, and she was a widow.

"What should she do if Robert should die? She was too feeble to work, and old age was fast creeping upon her. Kind neighbors had paid her expenses, and fitted her out comfortably, with the hope that she would be able to bring him home; for Robert was a good young man, and much respected.

"When we asked her in the morning respecting her son, she replied, 'Oh! he looks much brighter, and I think he can go home in a few days;' but, as we entered the room, those bright eyes bore the signal of death, and the sweet face had a heavenly expression; as the poor mother held the thin hand in hers, later on, he told her he was going home, where the others were, and it may not be long before *she*, too, will meet them. He died! and as they took his body to the dead-house, her agony seemed too great to bear; but, in the midst of all, the State agent came, and told her that she and her dear boy could be sent to Pennsylvania, and when she arrived at her own home, friends would go with her to his last resting place. Smiles mingled with tears, as she replied, 'Though He slay me, yet will I trust in Him; God is good, God is good.' —

"This hospital is becoming a hard place. My heart yearns for good, pure society, and I long to go home to my friends and kindred. I hope I shall not be needed long, and that the day is not far distant when we shall all 'come marching home,' feeling that God has given us the victory.

"What a day that will be to me after witnessing all I have here, and hearing from my brave soldiers the story of their privations and sufferings. I have three Tennessee boys, quite young, and to hear how they left their friends in the night, and had to travel always after dark, through woods, fording rivers, through cold and hunger; how they left brothers and friends dead on the road, for want of food and clothing, gives one the heartache. How little do friends at the North know what our soldiers are passing through!"

If the mothers who had sons at this time under Mrs. Pomroy's care could have seen her watchful solicitude for their welfare, we doubt not it would have saved many a heartache. Mother-like, the weak ones were her especial care. When they went to Washington for a holiday, they parted from her with anxious injunctions not to get led astray, and to come home on time. Seldom were her directions disobeyed, and but once did she have to send a boy to the guard-house for misconduct.

The case in hand was that of a Pennsylvania youth, who was brought in with a wound in the shoulder, where a ball had passed through. It was a very bad wound, and after having been confined to his room for several months, he wanted to go to Washington. His nurse gave him enough money to get a good beefsteak and a cup of coffee, and, knowing his weakness, begged him not to go near any drinking saloons, and not to smoke, and to be in on time, which was five o'clock.

He promised in good faith, and joined two or three steady companions, who were going the same way. Five o'clock came, but not the boy. His mates had come home, but had lost track of him.

Two hours later he came in, the worse for liquor, and very disorderly, but very penitent. He had fallen several times, his shoulder-blade had been shattered, and he was in great pain. His nurse was much distressed, but saw it was no time to talk to him.

"Go directly to bed," she said, "and I will shield you this once, but not again. When the surgeon comes round, shut your eyes and be asleep, else he will discover your condition and send you to the guard-house."

When the surgeon came round, the boy was snoring soundly, and the medicine was left for the nurse to administer. Then she washed and dressed his wounds, and bade him sleep for the night.

The next day he was himself; ashamed and penitent for his folly, and ready to receive with all humility the words his nurse had in store for him.

"Remember," she said, after much kind and faithful advice, "this is your first offence and I forgive it, but the next time you will go to the guard-house."

He had opportunity while lying on his bed of pain, to think of his widowed mother, whom he loved dearly, and to vow never to take the fatal glass again. As he got better and was able to be round, he helped in many ways about the hospital, and was a most excellent boy.

After three months had passed he begged his nurse to try him once more, and let him go to Washington. She at last consented; furnished him with enough of his money to get a good dinner, and he promised to be home all right. He did not come at five, and the nurse began to feel uneasy. She waited until six, when she heard him coming up the stairs, swearing at the boys and hardly able to stand from the effects of liquor.

He commenced to cry on seeing her, and begged her not to have him put in the guard-house. His arm was soaked in blood, where he had fallen and injured it, and he was in great distress. She told him it was impossible for her to shield him again, and bade him sit on the side of his bed until she could send for an officer. The poor fellow came and stood before her, begging for pity, but it was of no avail, and he was hurried away.

Twelve o'clock came, and the officer of the day on his rounds found Mrs. Pomroy up.

"Why, what are you sitting up for?" he said.

"I cannot sleep," she replied, "for thinking of my poor boy in the guard-house. Do let him come up, doctor! He is a poor, weak boy, and his wound needs dressing."

"Mrs. Pomroy," he said, "what makes you

love these boys so? I haven't any right to let him out, but it is the first time you've ever had to send one, and for your sake I'll do it; but if it reaches the surgeon's ears, I shall have to answer for it."

The culprit was brought in soon after, in a shivering condition, his wound dressed, then he was made warm with ginger and put to bed to sleep off his drunken stupor.

He stayed with Mrs. Pomroy many months after this. He got strong and went to Washington several times, but never again came home intoxicated. Nor when he went to Meridian Hill to join the Invalid Corps, did she ever have cause to sorrow over her Philadelphia boy.

It is not to be supposed that medicine was relied on to effect a cure where homesickness and depression was at the foundation of illness, as in many cases. The surgeons and nurses did their best to raise the spirits of the men, believing as a rule, that those who laughed most were surest of recovery.

One day the surgeon on the ward proposed to the nurses that the boys have a dance before going to bed. They all agreed to it, and a man was found who had a fiddle and could call off the dances. When the surgeon in charge was called on for his opinion, he said he not only gave his consent, but his hearty approval, as he thought the patients would be benefitted by it.

The dance commenced, and lasted from seven until nine. The surgeon on the ward stood in the door and smiled his approbation.

Now there were some of the inmates who got wonderfully limbered as the fun and the dancing proceeded, and among the number, some who had before been apparently too weak to walk from their bed to the window. The surgeon made a note of such, when he saw them stepping so briskly to the measure of the music, and danced them off to their regiments next day without further ado.

> To suffer well is well to serve;
> Safe in our Lord
> Divinest compensations come;
> Through thorns of judgment mercies bloom
> In sweet relief.

CHAPTER VIII.

FAITHFUL UNTO DEATH.

IN April, of the year 1864, the cry of our starved men in Southern prisons reached the ears of the President, and touched his sympathetic heart. Negotiations were entered into with the South for an exchange of prisoners, in consequence of which hundreds of starving men from Libby Prison, Andersonville, Belle Isle, and other places, were brought in as fast as the exchange could be made.

At Baltimore a hospital was improvised from a large old building on the wharf, built for the storage of grain, and given the name of West Hospital.

When these skeleton prisoners commenced to arrive, Miss Dix had orders from Secretary Stanton to secure Mrs. Pomroy's services for West Hospital, and she came to Columbia

College with tears streaming down her cheeks, to take Mrs. Pomroy and Mrs. R. to Baltimore. They were on their way in ten minutes, and at twelve o'clock reached their destination.

The oath of allegiance was administered outside, and again inside the outer door, with strict injunctions not to speak or even look at the rebel officers, through whose quarters they had to pass on their way to the Union men, who were on the second flight. Here again, the oath of allegiance was taken before entering. The sight that met their eyes as they passed in, beggars all description, but the details of the heart-rending condition of these poor sufferers have been so often depicted, that it needs no lengthy delineation at our hands.

Wild, staring eyes that met their gaze told the story of insanity. Their faces wore the hue of leather; their hair was filled with vermin, and their half-clad bodies covered with filth.

Weaker than new-born infants, many died while being taken from their stretchers. Still the stream of living death was poured in;

some through the door, others through windows, where elevators took them from the water side.

Every attention that medical skill could devise, every effort that faithful nurses could put forth, every luxury that the women of Baltimore could procure, was provided to fan the flame of life into a brighter glow; but all in vain for many. The oil was nearly burned; it flickered for a few brief moments, and then went out. Among the screams and groans which constantly assailed the ear, was heard the cry for mother, wife or sister; and dying blessings and the curses of the insane were mingled in one.

Mrs. Pomroy passed through these painful scenes, keeping up a brave heart and a steady hand until twelve o'clock at night. She had had nothing to eat since seven in the morning, nor could anything be obtained in the hospital. She felt her strength giving way, and knew that she must sink from exhaustion unless she could find a place of rest. She asked a soldier if he would tell her where she could find a bed. He said, "There are no preparations for sleeping here, but there is an empty bed in the attic, which has been vacated by a patient, and I will show you the way to it."

He took a half-burned tallow candle and showed her up the first landing. The steps were pieces of plank, one above the other, with no railing, and as she followed, with unsteady steps, by the dim light of the candle, she stumbled over something and almost fell.

"Oh, what is that?" she asked in agitation.

The man coolly informed her that was the dead body of a man just gone with spotted fever. "They are taking him out to bury," he said; "but don't be alarmed."

With increasing agitation, she passed up a second flight, where he led her into a large room, petitioned off into stalls, built for stowing grain, and there showed her the semblance of a bed, covered with a dirty quilt, and destitute of a pillow.

"This is the best I can do for you," he said, "but don't undress, for we have wharf-rats here, and they will eat up or carry off everything left about the room."

"Is there no way I can fasten the door?" she said, with nervous dread, looking around the barren apartment.

"No," he replied; "nothing will hurt you here; leave your candle burning till it goes out."

With that, he left her, and she recrossed the room and attempted to close the heavy door on its rusty hinges. The sudden sound woke a dreary echo in the room, when a wild voice cried out from the nearest stall, "Who's there?" Mrs. Pomroy answered with what feeble strength she had left, and asked in return, who the person was, and why they were there.

"Oh," said a woman's feeble voice, "what made you come here? Don't come near me. I am dying of small-pox."

Mrs. Pomroy waited to hear no more. Sinking by the side of her bed, she besought her Heavenly Father for strength and succor. Agonizing thoughts came thick and fast as she struggled in prayer. "What if I should be taken with the fever and die in this vile spot unknown, with no one to take me to Woodlawn and lay me beside my husband and children?" and then, "What would my dear friends at the North say, if they knew where I was to-night?"

In her distress, she prayed as never before, that if it was God's will, she might be kept from all harm, and live to be restored to home and friends, and when she arose and lay down upon her hard pallet, it was with a calm assurance that God knew all her distress of mind, that all things were in his hands, and that if he chose, he could bring her out of that foul room untainted by disease. Thereafter her mind was at rest. Exhausted nature kindly closed the weary eyelids, and she slept unmolested until the early dawn penetrated through the cobwebs on the windows and outlined the hugh rafters overhead.

When she arose she learned that the small-pox patient was still living, and that she was waited on by a colored man, who had had the disease, and who brought up her meals and medicine.

Leaving the room as soon as possible, she passed out of doors to the pump, near at hand, where she bathed face and hands and was greatly refreshed. The fears of the previous night were all dispelled, and inquiring for the nearest restaurant, she went in, bought herself a breakfast of steak and coffee, and was in condition to take upon herself the duties of nurse again.

For three weeks she occupied the same hard bed in the grain stall, the small-pox patient having been removed to another hospital, where she died the next day. Here she devoted herself in untiring service to the poor sufferers, save at intervals where change was a necessity. Now it was to administer a little weak gruel or a stimulant; again to quiet the ravings of the insane or idiotic; again to dress and bind up the frozen stumps of feet where gangrene had settled; and then to hear and transmit the last message to far-away friends and close the sightless eyes. One case especially worthy of notice, was that of a poor boy, little over twenty years of age, who had enlisted from Baltimore months before.

His father was one of the few Union men of that city, and when the Massachusetts troops marched through on that eventful nineteenth day of April, 1861, he had the courage to raise the Union flag. So much did this act incense the Secessionists, even his near friends, that they threatened to fire his beautiful residence if it was ever repeated.

Previous to this his family included four fine boys. Three of them died, and the stricken parents, irreconciled to their loss, rebelled against the afflictive hand of God. Time passed, and the remaining son, fired with his father's patriotism, joined the Union ranks, and with others, was afterwards taken prisoner. The parents learned where he was quartered, and sent sums of money and everything that heart could desire for his comfort while in prison. But nothing reached him. It went to feed the coffers and fill the mouths of the rebel guard. When the exchange of prisoners was made, he was brought to West Hospital, within two miles of his home. He was one of Mrs. Pomroy's patients, and on learning the facts of the case, she at once sent word to his parents that their son was in the hospital.

One day an elegant carriage drove up, occupied by a feeble old gentleman, who sent up his footman to inquire for Mrs. Pomroy. She went down to the carriage, and the father of her poor boy introduced himself.

Tears coursed down his cheeks as he asked, in faltering accents, for his son. "Can I see him?" he said.

"You can," said Mrs. Pomroy, "but you will find him greatly changed; you will not know him, and I must ask one favor, for your poor child's sake; do not let him see your distress by a single sign; it might cost him his life."

The old man promised. He was helped out of the carriage, and ascended to his son's room, leaning on the nurse's arm.

They went slowly on, passing one bed after another till they reached the one where lay a poor wreck of humanity, whose features bore no semblance to the once beautiful boy. "This is he," she said. The father started, gave a long look, then, with a wild cry, fell to the floor in a fit. He was taken to an empty cot, restoratives applied, and when partially recovered, his servants carried him to his carriage and took him home.

After this the mother desired to come. Mrs. Pomroy said, "Wait for a few days, till he gets stronger." Then the mother got permission to come and look upon her darling son. Tears fell like rain as she said, "In a land of plenty, with a rich father, and my *only son* dying of starvation!" And, "O, my Father, help me to bear this trial, for I never thought my poor boy would die for want of food."

He looked up, and said, "Be thankful, mother, that I die where the rebels will not throw my body where the dogs and rats may eat it."

But he did not die. Slowly the strength came back into those feeble limbs, and Mrs. Pomroy learned, weeks afterward, that he was restored to his parents, and that they lived to be reconciled to the loss of their other sons, and acknowledge God's mercy in saving them from sharing the same dreadful fate.

In the far corner of the sick room lay a poor little colored boy. He was dying of dropsy, and his swollen figure contrasted strangely with that of the skeleton forms around him.

"I'se most got home," he said, as Mrs. Pomroy came to feed him with a little weak broth. "I'se going home to see Jesus."

"Where are you from," she said, "and where did you hear about Jesus?"

"My home is in Car'lina, an' my mudder got 'ligion at de camp ground. We got separated, somehow, when de niggers set free, and she tell me, last ting, 'lub Jesus.'"

A sweet expression of love in death lit up his dark features and made them radiant. When next his nurse came round to give him another strengthening draught, and speak a word of comfort, he had reached home and Jesus.

Another choice young man from Philadelphia was slowly dying. He had much to live for. He had a beautiful home, and when he left, it was with the promise to marry a lovely young lady when the war was over. His distress was hard to witness. Mrs. Pomroy urged him to cast his troubles on the Lord. She told him the oft-repeated story of the thief on the cross, and urged him to pray.

"I can't pray," he said.

"Can't you say, Lord, remember me?"

And the poor fellow clasped his hands and repeated over and over, "Lord, remember me! Lord, remember me!" till death sealed his petition.

These are but a few cases out of the forty under her charge. Many a sad story might be written from the history of those woes, breathed only in her ear, but we will not harrow the feelings of our readers by any further recitals. Many got able to go home, and there, under its quiet influence, and the comforting ministry of friends, regained their health, and have become good and useful citizens, prizing the blessings of a stable government as never before. Others went home to join the vast army of patriots and martyrs of all ages, where "they shall hunger no more, neither thirst any more, and God shall wipe away all tears from their eyes."

In the room below where the Union men were cared for, were forty rebel officers, chained, waiting to be exchanged. They were surrounded by a double guard of officers, as one of the colonels had previously made his escape, though afterwards captured, on being wounded. Mrs. Pomroy passed through this room every time she went down stairs.

One day she looked up and met the gaze of one of these men, whom she thought she recognized. She asked the officer in charge if she might speak to him.

"Yes," he replied; "five minutes."

He accompanied her into the presence of the officer, and she said:

"Are you Mr. M., formerly of Chelsea?"

"Yes," he answered. "How, in God's name, came you down here?"

She replied, "I came to look after our poor wounded men. How came *you* here, and in such company?"

He told her he was fighting for his country; that he had espoused a just cause, and one that would triumph.

"Never!" said Mrs. Pomroy. "Never!"

"Why, just look at it!" he said. "Your men at the North are fast getting killed off, and there are none left who will fight."

"That is false," said Mrs. Pomroy, "and if it were true, I could go home and get hundreds of loyal women to take their places, rather than have our country given over to the mercy of the South."

This and much more he was forced to hear from her lips, while fierce hatred flashed from every feature, and he seemed almost unable to keep back his hand from striking her.

"Five minutes up," said the officer, and she left him to his own reflections, with a feeling, doubtless, of inward satisfaction that she had given the rebel officer a shot from the one weapon which women know how to wield.

While engaged at the hospital, Miss Dix called one day to take her away for rest and change. She had procured a pass for Fortress Monroe, and at five o'clock they were sailing down the Chesapeake, in the steamer *Georgianna*, bound for the Fortress, a distance of one hundred and eighty miles, and arrived there safely at eight in the morning. Their first stop was at the house of General Butler, who ordered his carriage to take them to the hospitals, a distance of four miles. Miss Dix was then to report their condition to him.

While passing from one hospital to another

they saw thousands of soldiers land. The great Army of the Potomac, swelled to one hundred and twenty thousand men, under Grant, was now about to move.

They visited a colored hospital, which was a novel sight. There lay our black soldiers, some wounded, others with fevers, and so on. One near the door attracted their attention. He was wounded, and three months before was wrecked, but clung to the mast five hours. When assistance came he joined his regiment, where, in a skirmish, a ball was fired at him, passing through his leg. He was happy; longed to get well and fight the Johnnys once more.

On the grounds near the hospital was a chapel which Boston had the name of putting there.

Mrs. Pomroy returned to duty among the sick and dying next day, and remained there till a despatch called her to Columbia College. From there she writes, May 24th:

"The recent battles have sent thousands of wounded men within the limits of our neighborhood. For the last ten days hundreds of ambulances and government teams have passed by our dwelling, and Carver Barracks, back of us, is crowded; so also Mount Pleasant and Stone Hospital, on our right. The first two or three days hundreds came to us who were slightly wounded. They had a good bath, clothes changed, their wounds nicely dressed, and were then sent to Northern hospitals.

"We were all day, for a number of days, dressing wounds, and trying to make the poor boys comfortable. . . . . We have now in our hospital over one thousand, many of whom are badly wounded. We have lost many by death, and the muffled drum, with its solemn notes, we hear several times a day.

"I never saw such patience among any set of men as I have among those who have been recently wounded. Not a murmur, nor scarcely a groan, is heard. The silent tear forces itself when I read to them, or show them my family photographs, and they seem very grateful for all that is done for them.

"On my right are two brave men who are shot through the face, the ball passing through the jaw, knocking out the teeth and cutting a piece off from the tongue. I can only understand them by gestures, as their mouths are badly cut. One of them carries round his teeth, and a part of his jaw-bone, in his pocket, as trophies.

"On the next four beds are those badly wounded through the right hand, and the next, a boy with his heel shot through, so that the nails of his boot pushed into the foot. It may have to be amputated. We have work enough before us this summer, and hope we have health to do all we can in times like these."

Strange as it may seem, Mrs Pomroy never had a soldier under her care who ever expressed a regret that he had enlisted. Large numbers of them were impatient to get well and join their regiments; but when homesickness seized upon the poor fellows, as it frequently did, it was impossible to rally their spirits or bring a smile into their wan faces.

One of her young patients had been sick several months, with no prospect of ever getting well, and he longed for home and mother. He begged his nurse to ask the surgeon if he could not have a furlough; he should get well if he could only see his mother. His request was refused by the surgeon; but he begged day by day, and two or three times a day, till at last Mrs. Pomroy herself importuned the doctor, telling him it was homesickness more than anything else, and that he might recover if sent home. The doctor finally consented, and the papers were made out. After waiting and expecting their arrival every day for weeks, and hope deferred had made the heart sick, the documents were put in his trembling fingers. But he could not read them, and gave them up to Mrs. Pomroy, saying, "You read them," which she did.

"Now you can go home," she said joyfully. "I will get you ready to-night."

A strange look came into his face; his eyes took on a dazed expression, where his nurse had looked for a glow of joy, and a moment after, he was raving in an insane frenzy, from which he never recovered. They took him to an insane asylum the next day, where he died, shortly after, a maniac.

June 12th, she writes in her journal. "Sunday: All is confusion and excitement; a large increase of wounded; many of them badly. June 13. Hands and heart full. Many of the wounded must die. June 14. Feeling worn out, and sick in bed. Doctors administered chloroform."

A few days afterwards she speaks of the loss of their matron, who had been with them two and a half years, and for whom the nurses had great regard. They presented her before leaving with a beautiful silver service as a testimonial of their affection. Having partially recovered in health, Miss Dix and the surgeon in charge invited Mrs. Pomroy to take the place of the former matron, urging her long acquaintance with hospital life and her fitness for the work; but she declined persistently, saying that her work was among the boys.

In July she writes: "On the Fourth, I went with one of the nurses to Georgetown, and from there crossed the canal and put my feet on the sacred soil of Virginia.

"The first thing that attracted my attention was a log house where our Union troops were stationed, and there hung Jeff Davis, large as life, in effigy. From there we went inside of Fort Corcoran, where the soldiers were delighted to see us, my companion being a New York lady. On learning that I was from Massachusetts, they concluded that I must be an Abolitionist."

One poor fellow from New York at this time took strong hold of her sympathy. He was brought from the field badly wounded, and was obliged to have his leg amputated. He was very sensitive about his loss, and would not let his nurse mention it in her letters. Often he would say, while tossing on his bed of pain, "If I could only see Sarah!"

Sarah was his wife — the mother of his little family of children — with whom he had sung many years in the choir of a small Methodist church in New York. His nurse saw that he was failing fast, and that he never would be able to go home to her, and, unbeknown to the surgeon, sent word that her husband wished to see her. On the next Saturday night she arrived, weary and faint, and Mrs. Pomroy gave the woman her own bed and supper.

On the following morning, after the doctor had made his usual call, and the husband was neatly dressed for the day, she told Mrs. M. that she could go in and see her husband, but charged her to let no outburst of feeling overpower her in his presence. She entered the room, and was led to the bedside of her husband, where the absence of his leg was plainly visible from under the thin sheet. Her agitation could not be concealed at first, but she grew calmer and sat down beside him, while Mrs. Pomroy took her seat upon the other side. They talked of the children for a while, and then he said, "Sarah, will you strike up one of the tunes we used to sing at home?"

With faltering accents, she began "Welcome, sweet day of rest," while the sufferer joined in, and the familiar strains were caught up here and there throughout the ward-room.

The poor woman ate her dinner in Mrs. Pomroy's room, with tears streaming down her face.

"Don't you think he will get well?" she asked.

Mrs. Pomroy informed her as gently as possible, that she must prepare to lose him, advised her to tell her husband and talk it all over with him. She went in and sat down beside him, and when she could quiet her emotion, she told him that she was afraid he could never recover.

He turned to his nurse and said, "What do you think, mother?"

Already her practised eye detected the seal of death on his brow. She could only confirm the intelligence his wife had imparted, and tell him he had but a little while longer to stay. He received the information calmly, told them he was willing and ready to go, and they talked of the future both for him and for her. Then he asked her to sing once more. Their voices blended in one as they joined in the dear old hymns they had so often sung together, till his, growing fainter and fainter, ceased altogether.

She was well nigh inconsolable when she became conscious that he had left her and he was carried out to be prepared for the simple pine coffin that awaited him.

Too poor to pay the expenses of his transfer home, Mrs. Pomroy procured her assistance through kind friends who visited the hospital, and she left in possession of his body, which was buried from the little Methodist church where he was known and loved so well.

Mrs. Pomroy at this time won the undying gratitude of another young man, by saving him from immediate death through neglect of medical treatment. He was brought in with a dreadful wound through the mouth. The ball had passed in on one side of the face, crushed the jaws, and taken off the end of his tongue, coming out the other side.

The surgeon looked at him and said, "No use to do anything for him, he can't live," and passed on.

Mrs. Pomroy stooped down and examined the poor fellow's wounds, and called her attendant, saying, "We can but try."

She took her instruments and picked out some teeth and pieces of bone, dressed his wounds as well as she could, for he was in great distress, and fed him like an infant. He could not speak so as to be understood, but on searching his pockets, they found the name Paul Kane, Boston. This, they learned, was the name of his brother, who was connected with the Revere House of that city.

She immediately wrote on to him, stating particulars, and saying that if he would forward some money she would see that it was expended in helping to restore his brother. The money was sent, together with many anxious inquiries for the son and brother. For days she fed him like a sick infant, plugged his wounds and dressed them, till he was finally able to sit up and be dressed, and then to walk about. Shortly after this he wanted a furlough. His nurse procured it for him and got him ready.

The surgeon who saw him after his first night's treatment, was surprised to find him so comfortable, but said it was of no use to spend any more time on him, and had taken no care whatever of him during these weeks of convalescence.

On the morning of his intended departure, however, he came in, and said, "Come, Kane, sit down and let me see your teeth."

"No, you don't," said the poor fellow; "you left me to die, and if it had not been for my good mother I should have been carried off where so many other boys are lying. Now you shall not look at my teeth. When I get to Boston I will get a dentist that knows something about the business, and I'll report you."

He started on his furlough, and not many days after Mrs. Pomroy took hers.

While in Boston, one day, she stepped into the Revere House, with a friend, and called for the porter, Paul Kane. A fine-looking fellow, of Irish descent, entered the room and received them politely.

"Have you a brother?" Mrs. Pomroy said.

"Oh, yes! He's a soldier just home from the hospital. He nearly lost his life, but a kind woman, a Massachusetts lady, was a mother to him, and saved him. Here are her letters, that I always carry about with me (taking them from his coat pocket). How I wish I could see that lady."

"You have the pleasure of seeing her, then," said Mrs. Pomroy, "for I am she."

The man started in astonishment.

"Can it be possible?" he exclaimed, seizing her hand. "Now I can thank you for all your kindness to my dear brother;" and the tears coursed down his manly cheeks.

Mrs. Pomroy then learned of her boy's safe arrival home, and some time after called at his home in Cambridgeport. But the struggle for life had been too much for him, and he was gone.

He did not live many weeks after his arrival home; but she had the satisfaction of knowing that he died among friends who kindly ministered to his every want and gave him a burial among his own kin.

>   Not painlessly doth God re-cast
>   And mould anew the nation:
>   Hot burns the fire
>   Where wrongs expire,
>   Nor spares the hand
>   That from the land
>   Uproots the ancient evil.

CHAPTER IX.

SHE HATH DONE WHAT SHE COULD.

ON this, her third furlough, Mrs. Pomroy was eagerly sought for by her friends, who vied with each other in providing every comfort for the recuperation of the frail, worn system that she was to get in readiness for another campaign. She inhaled the fresh mountain air of New Hampshire, among family friends, for a while, and, as before, spoke in public and private circles.

We cannot forbear, here, to give a brief sketch taken from the *Chelsea Telegraph and Pioneer*, of one memorable evening:

MRS. POMROY.— On Wednesday evening the City Hall was crowded to repletion, so great was the desire of our citizens to listen to Mrs. Pomroy's recital of her experience as hospital nurse in Washington during three years of the casualties of war, and the sufferings of our sick and wounded soldiers incident thereon.

Mayor Fitz presided, and introduced Mrs. Pomroy, who commenced by saying that she did not come before them as one of the strong-minded women, so called. She felt that she was among friends; friends to her, and to the soldiers of whom she purposed to speak, and among whom the experiences she had to relate occurred.

She then pursued for full an hour and a half a recital of hospital incidents connected with the wounded and sick soldiers; the sufferings, fortitude and love of country; their gratitude, their sorrows, hopes and fears; their fluctuations of mind and spirit while hovering between life and death, all delivered and delineated with such simplicity and modest grace, such pathos and devotion, as to make the narration one of the most interesting and instructive that can well be conceived of.

Tears rolled down many cheeks. The men wept as well as the women. The influence was profound. It was worth a score of sermons. It illustrated practically the great lesson of Christian duty. Mrs. Pomroy has been instrumental in saving many lives given over by the surgeons. By patient watching and care, by night and day, by the Great Physician, whose help she sought in prayer, she has had the satisfaction of seeing her sacrificing cares rewarded by perfect restoration of the patients. "Yes," said she, while relating one of these cases, "I saved his life. Yet not I, but God, for he told me what to do."

Indeed, all through her hour and a half discourse, she seemed like one not of the earth wholly. Her eyes but once or twice at most, met those of her audience; the lids were drooped; the tips of her fingers of one hand rested on, or moved with slow, unconscious motion, like one in thought, over the table at which she stood. Her voice was clear, modulated, low, utterance distinct and uninterrupted throughout.

There were no unnecessary words; no redundancy of detail. There was nothing boastful in all she said, all power of endurance being ascribed to a higher power.

A wounded boy was urged by her to pray. He said he could not, and then asked, "Do you pray?" "Yes," said she, "I could not stay here if I did not pray; prayer alone sustains me." The dying boy asked her to teach him. She told him the prayer of the thief on the cross. "Can't you say 'Remember me?'" He would try. He asked her then to pray with him, and taking the boy's hand in hers, she knelt and prayed with him.

Again, when ordered by Miss Dix to go to Baltimore to minister to the eight hundred Union soldiers then returned from Libby Prison, on seeing them in such a state of emaciated wretchedness, her heart sinks within her, and she exclaims, "O God! who is sufficient for these things?" But prayer brings strength, and with sustaining grace and faith she prosecutes her work.

Watching by a soldier's bed and reading to him, a secondary hemorrhage ensues. She presses her finger on the artery at the neck, and sends for the surgeon. There is some delay. The surgeon at length arrives, but the man sinks from the loss of blood which continues to ooze and drop from the amputated stump down at her feet. While pressing back the life current by her finger, she continued to speak words of encouragement and religious consolation to the dying man. Who, indeed, is sufficient for these things without help from Heaven?

Thus we see how the office of nurse is magnified by this, our excellent townswoman, to an exaltation not always attainable by those set apart for the office of spiritual guides and teachers. Mrs. Pomroy leaves for Washington on Monday or Tuesday next.

She writes to a friend on her return in September:

"I find myself once more settled down for the winter, after enjoying my pleasant visit home. The New Hampshire air gave me strength, and the little white cottage peeping out from among the trees welcomed me and bade me enter, where these nerves could be kept quiet and grow stronger. As I rode through the hilly country, I thought of the many brave boys from here that have been under my care, and almost wished I could see the friends of some of those who lie now in soldiers' graves.

"The first person I saw when I reached Washington was my good friend, the President; and I enjoyed a hearty shake of the hand. All my boys go for Lincoln, and I have no doubt he will be re-elected. I would like to give my vote.

"I have made one proselyte, and shall try to reason with some others, who hardly know where they stand, but who will go home on a furlough to vote. We are all excitement here over the election, and evenings the guns are fired for Lincoln, with fireworks and other demonstrations. Our city is well guarded, as in every little space you see a cavalry man on duty, and our forts have hundreds of soldiers to protect them.

"What a day that shall be when peace shall be declared, and we all 'come marching home!' I trust it is not far distant. .... Many of my boys have gone home on furloughs, so I have quite a small family to look after.

"There have been changes with nurses and surgeons, and our old nurses look careworn and anxious. There are now twenty nurses, eleven new ones having been added. I must not forget to tell you that we have had supplements to our ration-money, the sum of *six cents*, as provisions are much higher since the war began, making now twenty-six cents per day for our food; but there has been nothing added to our stipulated sum of forty cents for our labor.

"Last Sabbath we had a new chaplain, an Episcopalian, our other chaplain having been discharged from the service. He preached such a good sermon that I do believe we shall all like him very much, for he seems like a *live* Christian, and at our prayer-meetings the soldiers take a great interest. Our last one was like a little heaven below."

In October, she writes:

"Aunt Mary, from Mrs. Lincoln, called to have me go out to the Soldiers' Home and spend a few days with the family. She says that the President has had several threatening letters, his house is guarded all round the outside, and a private guard inside the house. He has for a long time had a cavalry guard to escort him from the Soldiers' Home to his office. I shall go there, but shall spend only a short time, as I cannot be spared longer. To-night I am to watch with our surgeon in charge, who is very sick. He is from New Hampshire, and a brother of Professor C., of the Normal School, Salem."

While in the President's family at this time she had occasion to make application to him in behalf of an afflicted father who was then living in C.

His son had been arrested and convicted for theft committed in a post-office, and had been sentenced to prison for a term of years. Long months had passed, and the young man was wasting away from the effects of confinement and distress of mind. The father sought Mrs. Pomroy out, as many another one had done, knowing her influence with the President, and besought her to make an appeal for him to Mr. Lincoln.

There were extenuating circumstances, he urged. His son was young, was led into the crime by a wicked companion, and it was his first offence. He had always been a good and dutiful son under the home roof, and his mother had lain prostrate on a bed of sickness since the fatal sentence.

Mrs. Pomroy reluctantly took the commission, for she had long felt unwilling to trouble the already overburdened executive with matters outside the weighty affairs of the nation.

He heard her story with his usual patience, and said:

"I will give attention to the case if you will bring me all the papers that have the evidence of the trial."

The necessary papers were taken to him and examined. He then sent for Mrs. Pomroy, and said:

"I am burdened with appeals like these, and I cannot say yes, always. Tell me what you would think it right to do if it were your own son."

Mrs. Pomroy felt the burden of responsibility in this critical case. In it was involved the sentence of life or death, apparently, for this poor young man, and she could not speak for the moment. Then she said:

"It is right for justice to be done, as I should want it in case of my own son, but does not this call for mercy too? He is young, it is his first offence; it may save his own life, and restore the health of his sick mother."

"It shall be as you desire," said the President, and at once gave his signature to the petition.

The overjoyed father could not find words to express the debt of gratitude he owed his benefactress, and hastened home with the welcome tidings.

The petitions and appeals to the President from government officials, from all sorts of persons wanting situations of trust, and from others in distress, were extremely burdensome, for their name was legion. They were ready to greet him on his office steps in the morning, and they thronged his carriage at night.

One day a half-crazy unfortunate from C., Daniel Pratt, "The great American traveller," who had been dodging in and out of anterooms for some days without avail, made a sudden raid upon the President, when he, with Mrs. Pomroy, had just stepped into his carriage. His petition was short and to the point. He wanted an office. "Consider," he said, "it was *my* vote that made you President."

At another time he was besieged by a foreign-looking individual for the same favor.

"What can you do?" said the President, in his quizzical fashion.

"I can speak seven different languages," said the man.

"It would be a better recommendation if you could speak *one* correctly. Drive on, William" (to the driver), and he was beyond the reach of his persecutor.

The most important event of the month of November was the re-election of Mr. Lincoln. Among all the exciting events of those stirring times, nothing caused so much agitation as this. The soldiers were wild with enthusiasm, and bonfires and illuminations were the order of the day in and around Washington. That this event "destroyed the last hope of the Rebellion was ere long made apparent; but the call for two hundred thousand more troops, by the President, closely following, looked to the waiting people and soldiers as though there was to be a renewed outlay of life and limb.

Still vast expeditions were being fitted out with stores of ammunitions. Still the great bakery in the basement of the Capitol poured out its daily supplies of steaming bread for thousands of soldiers, who took up the weary march where others had fallen by the way. Still the careworn nurses went their rounds, soothing the sick and comforting the sad with every scrap of encouraging news that could be gleaned from headquarters.

When the short and dreary days of November came on, there were cases of homesickness and discouragement that medicine had no cure for. One little Massachusetts boy came in very sick of typhoid. For weeks his life was despaired of. He had a sister and a widowed mother, and he was an only son.

He was in Mrs. Pomroy's ward, and she took great interest in him and wrote often to his widowed mother. The poor woman pleaded with his nurse that she would do her best to restore him to health, but, if otherwise ordered, desired that he might be prepared to meet her in Heaven. Many fervent prayers were offered at the hospital for the little Massachusetts boy, for he was quite a favorite. In a few weeks he was able to sit up, and shortly after to move round somewhat. But he did not seem to gain after that. He lost courage at the prospect of being confined in the hospital through a long winter.

One morning an order came from the surgeon in charge for all who were convalescent to be sent to another hospital, and Mrs. Pomroy's blue-eyed boy was among the number. She went about the packing of his books and clothing with great reluctance, and even told the surgeon on the ward that she thought him unable to take the walk, but he turned on her with the harsh reply, "He shall go now and *work*, for he has been petted too long here." Sadly she helped him on with his blue overcoat, gave him a farewell kiss as the drum beat, and among the convalescents as they marched away, she watched poor Henry.

Not quite an hour, and a noise was heard in the hall; they were bringing back her boy, sick and faint, and he was again put in his bed in the corner of the ward.

He failed rapidly now. A week before his death he had a letter from his little sister, saying she had been fattening a chicken and would send him a Thanksgiving box. He was much pleased, and asked if he could eat some of his Thanksgiving, and was told he might eat all that he was able. The night before he died, he asked his nurse if he might lean his head on her shoulder, for he could not rest anywhere. Then he said, "When I am gone, will you tell my other mother that I found her Saviour, that I was a good boy and minded all you said to me; that I should like to see her once more, but all is right?" Saying this, he breathed his last.

She cut off a lock of his hair, and sent it, with other little trinkets, to his sister, and placed beautiful flowers around his coffin before it was taken to the dead house.

As the litter on which he was taken was being carried down-stairs, it was stopped by a box coming up. It was the poor boy's Thanksgiving. His tearful nurse divided it among other patients, who ate it thankfully, not knowing from whence it came, while the dear boy, let us trust, was giving thanks that home was reached, and his warfare had been accomplished.

She writes in one of her letters that follows: "Among our number we have three wounded rebels, one whose under-jaw is smashed in, and the other two are wounded in the limbs. If they are sensitive, they must suffer in mind, as our boys will sing all the patriotic songs they can find, especially the *Rebel Flag.*

One of these men came under Mrs. Pomroy's care, though she begged to have him transferred, for, as she writes: "I could not feel right towards him after having seen those starved boys. He said he did not blame me at all, and seemed to feel himself at my mercy. I did not do the first thing until I had asked the Lord how to deal with him; how to win him over.

"I asked him why he joined the rebel service. He said he did not want to, but his father threatened to disinherit him if he did not; that he did not wish to kill any one, and that he never had. He joined the ambulance corps, and while taking the wounded rebels off the field, a ball went through his leg, and he fell."

After he had been in her care a few days, he wanted to know if he might call her "mother," like the other boys.

"No," she says; "not while you are cherishing rebellion in your heart towards our great and good government."

She writes again: "My rebel is now thinking of taking the oath of allegiance, and a good boy he is. He thinks much of me, and is excellent help; a good watcher, and very kind to my sickest ones. I tell him I am so sorry that I cannot call him *my boy*, and he laughs, and says I *am* his mother."

And again: "My rebel was a good young man, and before he left me, when we shook hands, the tears came to his eyes, and he told the boys that I was better than his mother at home, and that he should take the oath of allegiance before he left the hospital. The

Lord heard my prayer, for he felt not only that he had been fighting against the best government, but against God, and when he left me, he was a true penitent, waiting and willing to be led in the path of duty. The Lord go with him, and bless him, is my prayer."

Of the November election she writes: "My dear, kind friend Abraham is re-elected. I felt he would be, and such excitement! Our boys went to one of the torch-light processions, and my Massachusetts flag was carried by a colored sergeant, with only one arm. When the war is over, if that flag could tell the places it had been in, and the speeches it had received, it would be quite interesting. It graces the hall for concerts, temperance divisions, political speeches, and is frequently called for on the ground of its being a Massachusetts flag. I shall be proud to take it home with me when the war is over. . . .

"Our matron is not the one to fill such a responsible situation, and such troubles as we are having. I have never seen the like before since I came to the hospital.

"We shall have to make a change, as our

food is not half cooked, and the butter is worse than lard, so that I have eaten bread and molasses for the last three weeks."

In her next letter she writes: "Major C—— and Miss Dix have decided on my taking the matronship, but I have declined for the third time. I do not want so much care, for it is worse than keeping a boarding-house. There are twenty females to provide for, then nurses are sent here to remain till Miss Dix can find them places. Besides, there is so much to do with the sanitary rooms, State agents, and last, though not least, with inquisitive women who come to the hospital for reporters, etc. I like best to be with the boys, and they will not hear a word to my leaving the fourth floor. . . .

"We have been busy this week in whitewashing the building, and fixing up my ward with evergreens and roses for Christmas. The men are covering letters with red, white and blue tissue paper for various mottoes. In the centre is a picture of our good President, ornamented with a wreath; opposite him is General Grant; then I have had some pictures sent me from Boston, and *we look gay.* Should like to dine with you all on Christmas, and have a good sing in the evening. It is very cold weather, and snow is on the ground. I hope this will be my last winter here, for I am getting tired of war."

Mrs. Pomroy furnished entertainment for her charge on Christmas of this year, by instituting the time-honored custom of filling their stockings.

They had, the day before, been furnished each with a new supply of stockings from the North, and they were told they should find something in them next morning if they would hang them.

Accordingly, they were found suspended from bed-posts, chairs, and door-knobs, not one missing, when she and her attendant went the rounds that night after all had gone to sleep.

She had received a generous supply of candy, sent her from Copeland's, Boston, as had been done frequently before. This was put in cornucopias, with each soldier's name pinned on, and put inside his stocking.

When the boys found it the next morning

they were as pleased as the hundreds of little children were who were emptying the contents of theirs after the same fashion.

One old man, whose whitened locks bore the impress of nearly seventy years, wept like a child over his candy. He was a grandfather, with four sons in the war.

The image of little hands busy in rifling stockings that he used to fill, was haunting his memory, and was doubtless torturing him with the anxious inquiry: "Shall I ever see those dear, sweet faces again?"

It was amusing, that morning, to see how quickly the quid of tobacco was replaced by a tempting bit of candy, for those who wished it, had their allowance of tobacco, if money or friends could procure it for them. The use of the weed was second nature to some of these men. One old veteran came in with both arms shot off, and the attendant in charge was given the duty of cutting and preparing it for his daily use, and placing it in his mouth.

Another felt the craving for his stimulant in the dying hour. "Mother," he said, turning to Mrs. Pomroy, "can I have one more smoke?" His pipe, that had been his solace through many a rough campaign, was brought, made ready, and put between his lips; he gave two or three faint whiffs, and expired.

She writes in the month of December, after acknowledging the receipt of a box from Chelsea:

"I am kept busy all the time and hardly have a chance to think of home or friends. Oh, how much I do want to see this war at an end! My heart grows weary with the wrongs and sufferings, the trials that constantly rise up before me; but I know trials bring strength from above, and as my Saviour passed through suffering, I know he will sympathize. Sometimes I feel that I burden my friends with my troubles; but I will try and make the best of things, and as I do not believe in singing —

> Hark, from the tombs a doleful sound,

And as I am so constituted that I must be cheerful and happy, my song shall be —

> Thus far the Lord hath led me on.

"About my wants. All that you send, I appreciate highly. The wax was just the thing; the pan, pepper-box, etc., all right, and I feel quite grand every time I have what I need added to my *china closet*. I sometimes get tired of living in trunks, as I have for over three years, and the height of my ambition, when I come home to settle down, will be to have a room with a carpet and a bureau. So you see in my calm hours I am looking to the future and building castles.

"While I am writing you, the college bell is ringing loud for fire. The long ladder is here at my large window, ropes are thrown out, and the fire company with axes and buckets are shouting at the tops of their voices. We are not alarmed, for it is simply a play at fire. Some four weeks since an order came from the war department, that buckets, ropes, ladders and all the men who could handle them, must be used three times in a week, to practise, as they expected the college would be set on fire by the rebels. Strangers are not allowed in the hospital unless they have friends. Last Sabbath there were eleven called to see the Massachusetts nurse on the fourth floor."

The condition of her health at this time was undermining her strength, and evidently making her duties unusually tedious. She writes:

"I am much better now than when I last wrote you, and I am able to take my accustomed place at the nurses' table again, and administer some consolation to my poor, brave boys, not only in doing up their wounds, but in trying to lead them to a better life.

"Every severe attack I have helps to loosen the cords that bind me here; and whether the last cord will be snapped *here*, God knows best and knows only. I have committed all into his hands, knowing that he will do all things well. Dr. C—— says I need not do anything this winter in my ward but rest, and then, in the spring, I shall be able to do the same as ever. He and all the nurses are very kind, doing all they can for my comfort. I have a nice, warm room in which the sun shines brightly; but rest assured if I do not feel able to stay, I shall write you. Until then you can feel easy about me, knowing that I am gaining in health."

But it is evident that there was not much improvement physically. Her correspondence was in a great measure dropped, and her "new journal" ceased its record entirely. She acknowledges the receipt of boxes as usual, and in one of these letters writes:

"I have no time to make anything for myself. We have to sew two hours every day on the hospital clothing now, as we have so few patients. Of course we must keep employed all the time, or the *forty cents per day might be too much for us*, and government might grow poor.

"When you see Miss N., please thank her for that tea. How I do wish she could have seen the faces of the boys as I gave them a mug full! for when they have a poor dinner, and they look so sorrowful, my *tea-pot* is brought out; and often they say, 'That tea is worth a dollar.' . . . There is nothing new, but a heavy battle is expected. I hope it may be the last."

Her thoughts were often upon her good

friend, the President, in these perilous times, and she expresses a solicitude beyond that for anything else. She writes to a friend:

"My soul is in the Lincoln family, and why I am so distressed for them all God only knows. Sometimes I think God has put this heavy burden upon me for some wise purpose best known to himself. My heart cries out to God in behalf of Mrs. Lincoln and our dear, good President. I feel that I can pray for him hourly."

Soon after this letter was penned, came news of the fall of Richmond, and at the end of another week, tidings of Lee's surrender at Appomattox Court House was flashed through the land. The welcome news of "Peace" permeated every home and every hospital, and there was joy and tumult, laughter and weeping mingled in one loud pæan. But where was the nurse who was first to weep with those who wept, and rejoice with those who rejoiced? No word of exultant thankfulness was received from her by waiting friends. Prostrate on a bed of sickness, she was struggling for life, while those to whom she had given back life and strength, were exulting in the anticipation of exchanging these scenes of suffering for the reality of home comforts and enjoyments.

We have no record of all that passed in that room of suffering, save that she had the best of care, and that a nurse from Boston was sent for, and watched over her in the first stages of convalescence from typhoid.

Then came the news of the assassination of President Lincoln. From the highest pinnacle of joy, the nation was plunged into the deepest gulf of sorrow. The news penetrated the sick-room where she, who had been visited with dim forebodings of this dire calamity, felt its fulfillment as a personal bereavement, and at a time when least able to bear it.

With the strength born of a determined will, she resolved on seeing the face of her dear friend once more. She was made ready by careful hands, and was taken into the presence of death, and there added her tribute of tears to that of hundreds of others who looked upon their beloved friend with unspeakable sorrow and affection.

As soon as was practicable, she was taken

from the hospital, from which all the convalescent boys had now gone, who were able to be conveyed to their homes. These are the particulars incident to this event, written from the home of a friend in Newburgh, N. Y., where she was then resting on her journey home.

MAY 2, 1865.

MY DEAR MRS. F.: — Some weeks have elapsed since I last wrote you, and I felt for a few days that my hand might never hold the pen again; but God, who is wise and good, has once more given me health, and this morning I am feeling well.

I am in a very pleasant home, where everything is being done for me, and since I have left the hospital I have gained rapidly.

I will not attempt to describe all I passed through in my sickness while there, but the sudden death of my dear friend, the President, then the threatened burning of Columbia College and the shooting of our pickets, one of whom was brought into the hospital — these, with other things which I will describe when I see you, all helped to keep my nerves in a constant state of excitement. But, thanks to my Heavenly Father, I can still feel "He doeth all things well."

On the twentieth of April I took my honorable discharge from the hospital, where I had cared for over seven hundred patients, and closed the dying eyes of nearly eighty. Miss Dix said she had not words to express her grief at my leaving the service, feeling, as she said, as though she was to be left alone with so much on her mind, and wishing I was only able to go to Secretary Seward's and dress the wounds of the whole family. She urged me to stay in the service and do nothing but rest for a few weeks, but the surgeon on my ward told me that I was doing a great injury to myself to remain any longer, so I think I will rest till Providence opens another place.

My heart ached as I saw the tears from my poor sick boys fall:

but I had served three years and seven months, and I felt that I must go. Two of my boys carried me down stairs in their arms, and expressed much sorrow at my leaving.

Taking all things, I have passed through trying scenes, but this morning the sun shines just as bright as ever, God is still good to us, and may it never be in my heart to complain or murmur while my experience is so full of God's unbounded love. To-day I expect to go to Catskill, and in June I hope to be at home if I am perfectly well, but shall not come home sick.

It is needless to say that she was welcomed home with open arms, and the rest so much needed was found in the homes of friends. Who can tell, if her good friend the President had lived, how different the leadings of Providence might have been at this time? But all the generous promises of ample remuneration and support which he guaranteed her were rendered void through his sudden death.

At the end of two years she found herself equal once more to the responsible duties of life, and accepted a position as matron of a reformatory home for girls, at Newton Centre, Mass. Here she remained for seven years, when the Home was disbanded, leaving her with four friendless little girls, for whom she desired to make a home.

Kind friends came to her assistance, and

this little family became the nucleus of what is now an institution incorporated under the name of "The Newton Home for Orphan and Destitute Girls," where she is still engaged in the work of blessing the lives of the unfortunate.

'Tis fully known to One, by us yet dimly seen,
  The blessing thou *hast been;*
Yet speaks the silent love of many a mourning heart
  The blessing that thou *art,*
While traced on coming years, in faith and hope we see
  A blessing thou *shalt be;*
Then here in holy labor, there in holier rest,
  Blessing, thou shalt be blessed.